No Restraints:
An Anthology of Disability Culture in Philadelphia

New City Press
Liberty Resources, Inc.

2002

No Restraints: An Anthology of Disability Culture in Philadelphia
Gil Ott, Editor
Contents © 2002, New City Press
All rights revert to contributors upon publication.
"Defying Invisibility" © 2001, Victoria A. Brownworth

Book design by Gil Ott / Singing Horse

ISBN 0-9712996-2-5

Published by: New City Press
           August Tarrier, General Editor
           1114 W. Berks Street
           10th Floor Anderson Hall
           Philadelphia   PA   19122
           215-204-7347
           www.temple.edu/newcitypress

Copies of *No Restraints* are available at discount for educational purposes. For information, contact New City Press.

No
Restraints:
An Anthology of
Disability Culture
in Philadelphia

Edited by Gil Ott

New City Press
Liberty Resources
2002

Contents

What It Is

An Introduction, by Gil Ott

Like any identifier, "Disability" is something a person must accept, must, in fact, reinvent for oneself in order to join its determined community. This self-nominating process is more pronounced for those of us with hidden disabilities, since it is the visual signifiers of disability which activate the social stereotypes which make, for those with visible disabilities, self-nomination moot. But even for those so stigmatized, membership is not a given; consider Christopher Reeve, who insists that he will not accept, but will overcome his paralysis.

In society, stigma's operation tends to isolate. In the case of disability, isolation is doubly reinforced; the non-disabled do not know how to transcend their reactive fears and charitable impulses, and the Person with a Disability is locked within the particularities of his or her own condition. Given these pervasive disincentives, it is truly wonderful that more and more individuals are declaring their disabled status as participants, both in the broader American community, and in that specific to their "otherness."

It is this active self-identification which transforms a benign social category into a political and cultural force, a community. If the Twentieth Century in America has been the Century of Civil Rights, it is not surprising that Disability Pride should follow Black Power, Women's Rights, Gay Pride and other collective bids for empowerment and integration. What characterizes every one of these movements is their proposal of a mechanism to resolve alienation through acceptance and redefinition of what had been a stigma, and which then becomes a criterion for membership in the group. In every case, advocates have dismissed stereotypes of moral or physical weakness attributed to their group, and have demonstrated that those very characteristics that had been considered weak are, in fact, sources of great individual and collective strength.

These communities are called "movements" for a good reason. Once they have declared their alignment, their members must continue to move, that is, to demonstrate and re-demonstrate that alignment for a majority society which would prefer to remain ignorant, idle, and entrenched. The record of such demonstration, performed individually or collectively, becomes available to all members of the group. It forms the basis of a distinct subculture.

The form of such demonstration can be as diverse as the group's membership. It is specific to, and, in a way, antithetical to, the very identifiers which determine the group, and it bears that contradiction forward like a banner. For some, an aggressive ownership of this contradiction is itself an emblem of distinction, one forbidden to those outside the group. In the case of the community of People with Disabilities, terms like "crip" or "gimp" signify membership beyond the reach of the able-bodied world.

Of the several Civil Rights movements active in America today, the Disability Rights movement is perhaps the most complex. The very coherence of "disability" as a broad category is often challenged, both from within and without the community. The Deaf and Blind communities, for instance, each have their own distinct histories and institutions, as do several chronic conditions, such as muscular dystrophy and multiple sclerosis. Other groups, such as People Living with AIDS/HIV, have only recently realized their status as People with Disabilities. In fact, the tendency continues for disability-specific groups to organize outside of the rubric of Disability, to present their particular cases to the American public. What is it, then, which unifies the entire field of Disability?

This question is at the root of this Anthology. By defining Disability as "any condition which limits a major life function," the Americans with Disabilities Act (ADA) drew a very wide and inclusive border around the community of People with Disabilities, a border so broad that no one has yet found it. In effect, this ADA definition has left the defining up to subsequent social and political refinement. Litigation is only the most tangible course of this refining process; of far greater importance is the cultural process, the multitude of ways in which individuals and small groups declare and assert their membership and belief in the community of People with Disabilities.

In gathering material for this Anthology, the operative definition of culture has been the broader, social and political one, and not exclusively the narrower, artistic one. What these definitions have in common, however, is their reliance on creative solutions to problems of identity and communication. Viewed in this way, protest becomes art, and art, so far as it participates in the values common to the group, becomes political statement.

Culture can be interpreted to include virtually every arena of human endeavor, as can Disability Culture. Athletics, fashion, business, spirituality, psychology and all forms of social interaction, all are particularly nuanced within the community of People with Disabilities. Viewed critically, Disability Culture becomes an evolving system of codes lacing together the difficult fabric of integration and specific identity.

In assembling this Anthology, there has been no attempt to be comprehensive. Since New City Press and Liberty Resources are located in Philadelphia, Philadelphia became a geographic determinant. Philadelphia's perspective on Disability Culture has its own flavor, determined by the issues specific to our city, and by the personalities and organizations unique to it. Furthermore, Liberty Resources is an advocacy-centered organization, so recruitment of writers and artists has proceeded through the network of activists and community members, and not academics or other professionals. What may be lost in objectivity is far compensated by the open-ended urgency of community-building and culture-making at the speed of life.

What has resulted is a snapshot of a dynamic culture in motion. Because a culture is both a collective and an individual thing, there has been no attempt to square divergent viewpoints. At all points, *No Restraints*, which takes its name from the struggle for humane treatment of psychiatric patients, has opted for individual representation over unified group portrayal. Some contributors address Disability as subject matter, while others are simply Artists with Disabilities. Also, there are noticeable gaps in these contents; Philadelphia is a national leader in Disability Rights, and has produced a varied contribution to its culture. One anticipates that *No Restraints* is only a first compilation of its type, both locally, and nationally.

The publication of *No Restraints* takes advantage of a fortuitous convergence of individuals and organizations, some of whom I would like to acknowledge here. Steve Parks, August Tarrier, and Nicole Meyenberg make up the staff of New City Press, which is founded on the vision that Philadelphia's community groups, given the means to produce their own books, will create a new, truly transformative literature. At Liberty Resources, President Fern Moskowitz and Deputy Assistant Director Linda Richman, as well as Erik von Schmetterling and other members of the Board of Directors, recognized early on the importance of this project, and gave it their backing. Also, Carol Wisker, Director of Accessible Programs at the Philadelphia Museum of Art, supported the Anthology from its inception through its publication launch.

Compilation of *No Restraints* began with discussions among an Editorial Committee, which included, along with myself, Leslie Fredericks, Barbara Gregson, Jessie Jane Lewis, and Joanne Marinelli. Many others contributed in many ways, including Steven Brown (Institute for Disability Culture), Joyce Burd (ArtReach), Jennifer Burnett, Eli Goldblatt, Cassie James, Solomon Jones, Bethany Meadows, Connie Schuster (Artists for Recovery), and Deborah Scoblionkov. The true "community" that put this Anthology together, however, is the group of artists, activists, and writers who have contributed their work and their time to make sure that this collection truly represents Disability Culture today.

It is a tribute to the strength of the idea of Civil Rights in America that the Movement for Disability Rights has emerged. Here is a movement that cuts across the accustomed boundaries of prejudice, the very determinants of movements based on skin color, gender, or sexual orientation. To a great extent, this Movement is new, and its membership daily reinvents itself. Its various parts work continually to find how they might fit together. It is in this fertile growing stage that shared values, expressed as elements of a nascent culture, are of great importance. In *No Restraints*, we are here, together, at the beginning of Disability Culture.

What Is Disability?

Erik von Schmetterling, M. D.

Most people in society see Disability only in terms of cure. Many think People with Disabilities should copy able-bodied persons or act like "normal" people. When disabled people *try* to live as "normal" people, we are called "inspirational," "brave," or "courageous." That is the only time we are good enough to be noticed. Otherwise, we are seen as being angry because we are disabled. Those who try to act "normal" are said to have "overcome" their disability! Of course, *no one* can overcome a condition of nature. Rather, People with Disabilities adjust to their disabilities, like all people do with many of life's conditions – adverse or otherwise.

The overall reaction to Disability by able-bodied society is one of fear and avoidance. Disabled People have been isolated, sheltered or institutionalized because many find it easier to deal with us by *not* dealing with us! Moreover, most people do not regard us as contributors *to* society. We are seen only as burdens. Disabled People are medicalized by society; people see us as being sick, and since there is something "wrong" with us, we are seen as helpless and hopeless. Consequently, we are also infantilized, no matter our true chronological age. Through such perceptions, we are robbed of our civil rights and our dignity as human beings.

Society forgets that *all* human beings need to be taken care of at some point or another in their lives; sometimes, at many points. What human being is not limited in some way? No one can do it all. Any person can be weak or vulnerable in any given situation – and a person can be strong in other given situations. Disability, then, is a cultural difference – as defined by our common experience, our strengths and our hopes as a people.

As such, then, disability becomes a natural condition of life. Most of us do not want to be cured or become the same as able-bodied people. We are different and some of us are proud of that difference. We are proud of our people's history. Disability Pride is an attitude few non-disabled people can fathom; it makes people very uncomfortable to think that someone could be grateful – or even happy and proud – to have a disability.

People with Disabilities are a cultural minority; and, like other minorities, we share common bonds of having been oppressed, stigmatized and discriminated against. A very real problem for us, however, is that few non-disabled people – even those who have experienced discrimination themselves – see our struggles as a civil rights issue. Too many do not recognize the need to understand – or even follow – those legal rights that we have already won.

That prejudice has created the oppression and discrimination that rule the lives of People with Disabilities today. It is evident in the fact that 1.7 million People with Disabilities are forced to live in institutions – nursing homes, state hospitals, residential schools, and other such long-term facilities. It is seen in the overall lack of available, affordable, accessible housing, thus keeping more of our people locked up in institutions. And, it is clearly seen in the remaining presence of many architectural barriers that persist eleven years after the passage of the Americans with Disabilities Act. Since its passage, the ADA has repeatedly weathered attacks; this past year a court case challenged the ADA, claiming it wasn't even constitutional; another Congressional effort is to force advance notification to ADA violators that would nullify the ADA's enforcibility. A severe backlash of resentment against the ADA continues to threaten its very existence.

Negative – even hostile – attitudes, i.e., pity or the belief in benevolent euthanasia, continue to pervade our nation. Such movements as the "Right to Die" or "Death with Dignity" campaigns, along with the prevalent Telethon mentality, offer us this choice: wallow in pity, or die. Pity has been called a "benign form of hatred" by Dr. Paul Langmore of UCLA, though hatred can never be truly benign. These movements illustrate this profoundly, because they end in the deaths of People with Disabilities.

THE HISTORY OF DISABILITY

Due to societal fear, People with Disabilities have always been kept isolated. In a few select cultures, we were elevated to the realm of gods or gods' messengers, i.e., shaman. In most societies, however, we were outright murdered, as disabled babies were thought to possess evil spirits or demons. In other cultures, disability was seen as a conveyor of karma – the sins of the past personified through individual difference.

It wasn't until the early nineteenth century that People with Disabilities first achieved a modicum of independence. This was not yet a class of people, however, but a few brave "oddities" who ran away to freak shows and circuses, and were able to live their lives economically free. It was also around this time that the concept of euthanasia begin to gain favor within the United States.

In the aftermath of World War I, the Nazi Party in Germany arose and assumed power there. The Nazi concept of the Perfect Man or "Über-Mann" was not congruent with disability. People with Disabilities were viewed as "useless eaters," as living "lives unworthy of life." The Nazis developed a program to exterminate first people with mental Disabilities and later all Disabilities, called T-4. Children and adults with all types of disabilities were murdered in German psychiatric facilities across their nation. Over 300,000 persons with Disabilities became the guinea pigs on whom the Nazis perfected and practiced their killing techniques, to be used later on other victims of the Holocaust.

During the 1930's and into the Second World War, Franklin Delano Roosevelt led the United States from a wheelchair for most of his term. However, to achieve his popularity and political goals, he had to hide his disability from the general public. Even as President, he could ill afford to be seen as weak or vulnerable. Ironically, during his presidential tenure, the White House was made completely wheelchair accessible, only to be rendered inaccessible once again upon his death.

It wasn't until the turbulent sixties that the breath of freedom began to be felt by a few People with Disabilities. Persons like Ed Roberts, Judith Heumann, Justin Dart, and Wade Blank began to realize the similarities within the dynamics of oppression. For Ed, who is called the Father of the Independent Living Movement, the call to arms was the simple want of a decent education. But no one with a significant Disability had ever been college-educated before. Ed's resourcefulness became Independent Living.

Judith did receive a college education in New York, but was not allowed to use what she had earned: her teaching credential. She was told that no school building was accessible, so she couldn't teach. Outraged, Julie went on to found Disabled In Action of New York City.

It was Wade Blank – cofounder of ADAPT – who put it all together. Wade was an able-bodied person and a peace activist, which gave him a perspective not seen before by Disability Rights advocates. He was the one who connected the struggles of various minorities, and who saw the bonds that should bind.

Throughout the 1970's, independent living centers (CILs) exploded onto the American scene. First was Berkeley, California, then the Atlantis Community in Denver, Colorado, with many more following in their wake. Our movement grew out of the proliferation of CILs during the 1970's. For a center to be qualified as a CIL, advocacy must be one of four core pursuits. CILs can be described as being the center of our Movement, like the Black Churches of the 50's and 60's were for the Civil Rights Movement.

In 1973, the National Rehabilitation Act was passed, though it took four years for the final regulations of that law to be written. In April 1977, protests across America — some lasting a day, to one in San Francisco where Disability Rights activists occupied the Federal Building for almost a month. Finally, President Jimmy Carter relented and agreed to have the regulations written. Nevertheless, the housing portion of those regulations were not finished until 1988, when they were submitted to the US Congress by HUD.

THE DISABILITY RIGHTS MOVEMENT

Leaders of the Movement strongly felt that in order for our People to be free, we must be able to travel about freely and independently. Without the ability to get anywhere, we would accomplish nothing else. Hence, the fight for accessible public transportation became our battle cry. For years, civil rights organizers have seen the importance of equality in terms of being able to ride mass transit. This is the essence of what inspired the Montgomery Bus Boycott – restricting where certain people could sit on the bus affected their abilities to get to work on time. A people's outrage and anger became the Civil Movement. Not being able to ride buses, subways or other elements of a system's fixed route angers People with Disabilities, too.

The typical response has been to delegate People with Disabilities to use paratransit. That was to be our alternative. However, separate is *never* equal, and our People are not content with *just* paratransit. The passage of the Americans with Disabilities Act (ADA) on July 26, 1990, changed this discrimination forever by guaranteeing People with Disabilities the right to access all forms of public transportation. It was a long, hard fight – twelve years in the realization, but its success is paramount to all other endeavors.

As the struggle continues – now for *real choice* – organizers are seeing our Fight as points of a triangle: accessible transportation/community services/accessible, affordable housing. Without one, one can't have the others; lose one corner and the triangle falls apart.

Once the ADA became law, the Disability Rights Movement went head-to-head with the medical model. We went back to our roots, so to speak. Most – if not all – People with Disabilities, at one point or another, are in dire jeopardy of becoming institutionalized, usually in a nursing home. This is the result of antiquated federal mandates (Medicaid) and the institutional bias they create. All for the want of needing help to get up in the morning, bathed, dressed, and fed.

These are not medical services – no one requires a medical degree to perform them. Yet, society is paying through the nose to provide such services within institutional settings. All to the profit of the nursing home industry and medical communities. Furthermore, this medicalization of disability appeases societal fears and prejudices.

The struggle now lies in shifting the current federal mandate from nursing home placement to providing a choice to individuals who are in need of such services. If an individual chooses to go into a nursing home, he or she can. But if – like most people – they choose to remain in their own homes and receive their services there, the shifted mandate would allow that. The shifted mandate is in the form of federal legislation before the 107th Congress, called MiCASSA – Medicaid Community Attendant Services and Supports Act. It was introduced on August 1, 2001 in the US Senate by Senators Arlen

Specter [R-PA] and Tom Harkin [D-IA].

The campaign for MiCASSA has been an even tougher struggle than for accessible transportation, though the societal fears, prejudices and stereotypes that pervade all of these issues remain staunchly entrenched. We have gone up against some very powerful enemies, including the American Health Care Association, the American Nurses Association and the American Medical Association. We have teed-off against the medical model itself. Our main challenge has been to make people realize that People with Disabilities have been victimized by society's perceived roles of us – *not by our Disabilities*! Old attitudes die hard and this one seems particularly resilient. However, we must succeed or the backlashes will chip away at our hard won victories until we're right back in the institutions.

Yet even this is not enough! Only through hardcore activism – in the streets – will we ultimately win our final victory. There are many types of activism; not every single Disabled Person has to be out there in the street. We need everyone in this fight. We cannot relent, either because of our own fears or distaste for specific styles. Only one style is mandatory and that is: to do SOMETHING and to do it non-violently!

Defying Invisibility

Victoria A. Brownworth

We hear the term all the time: "Coming out." It used to refer solely to the declaration of being queer. Now it refers to acknowledgement of any previously hidden aspect of one's self. It is a declaration of one's visibility.

I came out as a lesbian in my freshman year of high school. I came out as a crip thirty years later, after being diagnosed with Multiple Sclerosis. There was no sudden moment of discovery of my lesbian identity and no concomitant revolt against it. As I imagine heterosexual women never have a declarative moment of realizing they have accepted membership into the sexual majority, I never questioned the rightness of my lesbianism; any conflicts I have had over my sexual orientation have come from social pressure to be straight, not from an internal desire to be so. I have never really desired to be anything other than lesbian.

But unlike acknowledgement of my lesbianism, the discovery that I was disabled, that I would not recover, came as a tremendous, unwelcome shock. I struggled against acceptance of my disabled status, much, I suppose, as many a queer struggles against acknowledging her or his sexual status. But all such struggles are ultimately as futile as they are painful. There are inherent aspects of who we are that defy transcendence.

Social and cultural marginalization are never

choices made willingly, yet few of us thrust onto those cultural margins have options. We cannot choose our race, gender, ethnicity or sexual orientation. Nor can we choose whether or not to be disabled; nearly all that disables the human body, either in the womb or after, is beyond our control.

I don't believe I chose to be a lesbian; lesbianism has always seemed innate while all efforts at heterosexuality seemed contrived. I did, however, choose to "accept" my sexual identity, rather than deny it. Conversely, I have struggled to accept my disability, a struggle surprisingly arduous and continual.

Activism is often an accident of timing. I was fortunate to have awakened to my lesbianism at the same time the queer nation was being jolted into action by the Stonewall Rebellion. There was no such confluence for my acknowledgement of disability. My carefully constructed, politically conscious activist life included friends of all races, ethnicities, religions and classes—and not a single close friend who was disabled. Were the disabled as invisible to me when I was nondisabled as queers were invisible to straights?

The enforced invisibility of the disabled parallels the enforced invisibility of queers. Marginalized, in closets not of our making, we are often asked why we demand visibility, why we must "flaunt" ourselves. Despised by a majority culture (straight, nondisabled) of which we are marginal members, we are expected to be self-loathing – and as a consequence be covert, remain hidden.

Visible for so many years, I cannot accept invisibility now. I learned early that visibility forces change. The lesson of the Stonewall Rebellion taught me; the women and men who augured that political conflagration were mentors to what became for me a life of queer activism.

I know how to be a lesbian activist because I have been one for thirty years. Disability activism is more difficult. I navigate a territory for which I have no map. Catapulted into the newly demarcated landscape of lesbian visibility when I was very young, I learned the topography early, sought out the maps and charts, became a geographer of that world.

As I search for images of disability, for writings by disabled writers, for a history of disabled life, I find a crushing similarity between these early days of disability rights activism and the early days of queer activism decades ago. Just as I had searched the library shelves as a teenager for models of lesbianism and found none to which I could relate, I have found little within existing disability literature to help me model myself as a disabled lesbian. (As of 1999 not a single book on lesbians and disability had been published in the U.S. In 2000, my book *Restricted Access* became the first.)

The disability model — like the early lesbian model — is based on a stereotype created by those who aren't. That is, as the narrow definition of lesbianism was defined by straights, so too is the narrow definition of disabled defined by nondisabled. When I came out, lesbian literature was largely written along a medical model by straight male writers. Other books incorporated an internally homophobic pessimism that left no room for a positive future for a young lesbian like myself.

The majority of the non-academic writing on disability has a similar tone to those early days of queer literature. It remains voyeuristic and heroic — stories told along the 19th century Dickensian model of The Good Cripple. As Radclyffe Hall's Stephen Gordon was the heroic and self-abnegating lesbian "invert" in the classic novel *The Well of Loneliness*, Tiny Tim is the prototype of the Good Cripple in Charles Dickens's *A Christmas Carol.*

In this imaging of disability, the restrictions and limitations loom larger than do steps in front of a wheelchair. I want to blast away these presumptions about disability as I have preconceptions of lesbianism. I want different models to follow than that of the Good Cripple, epitomized with Superman-sized self-loathing in real life by Chistopher Reeve, because that model is as unworkable as the model of the self-loathing lesbian evoked in Hall's novel.

Disability sneaked into my life unexpectedly, uninvited, unwelcome. Unlike my lesbian identity, which I have worn comfortably my entire adult life, my identity as a disabled woman feels awkward, like a garment that doesn't quite fit properly, yet for which I have no tools with which to make alterations. Yet that discomfiture must also be made visible, because tales told of disability are all of heroic acceptance, miraculous cure, tear-jerking sentimentality, triumph over adversity. Disability remains something the nondisabled shudder over while mouthing the words "There-but-for-the-grace-of-God-go-I"; a marker for what they believe they can or cannot do, as in "I could never live like you" or "I would kill myself if I thought I'd have to spend life in a wheelchair."

These are insults: assimilationist concepts that presume disabled life – like queer life – beyond the realm of choice. As I have heard the repeated refrain "Who would choose to be queer?" the disabled hear a similar chorus: "How can you live like that?" As if we have an alternative. As I refuted a straight image of lesbian identity, I refuse this limited notion of disability.

The link between disability issues and queer struggle reprises every day. For decades I have been asked by straights why I flaunt my lesbian identity. I am now asked this about my disability. Why must I make an issue of it? As if to say, "Must you call attention to it by trying to get in where you have been deliberately excluded by inaccessibility?" For three decades I have been asked why I can't simply pass for straight — after all, I am told, I don't "look" like a lesbian. And straight society would be much more comfortable if I would keep my lesbianism invisible. Now I am asked to adjust the comfort zone of the nondisabled by pretending my disability doesn't exist – which means, unlike "passing" for straight, where I am merely expected to keep silent about my sexuality, I must literally become invisible, disappear, because my disabled body cannot "pass" for nondisabled any longer.

Real-life lesbianism isn't a glamorously staged *Penthouse* magazine fantasy photo spread; its very ordinariness, so unlike the exotic pornographic portraits, unnerves straight society because "we" are too much like "them." Real-life disability reminds the nondisabled that they may be one car accident, one chromosome, one faulty gene away from a body that no longer works.

The disabled, like queers, are supposed to be silent, shamed, self-loathing, repentant. Queers and the disabled are supposed to accept their Otherness but never expect those who aren't Other to accept them. As a lesbian I shun assimilation, abhor tolerance. Assimilation is only as good as the people in power at any given moment; tolerance is forever being mistaken – dangerously — for justice. Disabled, I also shun these things. Experience has taught me we protect ourselves not with silence and invisibility but with resounding presence.

I am wary of tolerance. Assimilation looks remarkably similar to the closet to me. I have had the opportunity to pass for straight my whole life and have chosen not to. Why should I subvert who I am to make others comfortable?

Those of us who are Other in this society, those of us who have been made not cultural icons but cultural anathema have been diminished, minimized, demonized and even institutionalized as a way of making us disappear, making us invisible. But I choose not to be silent, I choose to flaunt. I choose to use my writer's voice, my activist history to break silences, refute invisibility. The shape and demeanor of my presence may have altered through disability. My politics have not.

The nondisabled can choose to see not me, only my wheelchair. But I can still block the path of their ignorance with my political presence, trip them up in their presumptions about disability with the words this Not-So-Good Cripple continues to wield as well as she did before disability struck. I may still be trying to fit this new garment of disability on my previously nondisabled body. I may have lost my physical strength. But I have not lost the power and intensity of my writer's voice. The nondisabled may not acknowledge my crippled self any more than straight society acknowledged my lesbian self, but that does not, cannot, make me invisible. Only my own silence can do that.

ADAPT Action Portfolio

Photography by Rodney Atienza

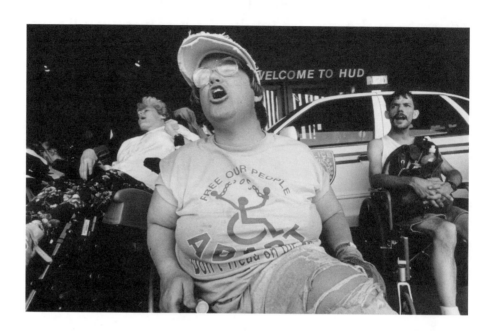

ADAPT is among the most vocal proponents of Disability Rights. Its members have learned to turn the public's fear of disability to their advantage, shutting down offices and conveyances with their very bodies and wheelchairs. Philadelphia-based photographer Rodney Atienza has captured the determination and passion of this culture of protest on film.

When Greyhound Bus Lines resisted implementa-
tion of the ADA, ADAPT chapters across the US
responded with firm, coordinated protest. In
Philadelphia, Cassie James led actions which
blocked bus routes and forced compliance.

Spitfire Sabel at the Greyhound action.

Erik Von Schmetterling.

Karen Burrison (center) and Cassie James block the bus.

When Princeton University hired Peter Singer, a proponent of "mercy killing" of People with Disabilities, ADAPT joined the anti-euthanasia group Not Dead Yet to protest the appointment.

One of ADAPT's primary goals is the passage of MICASSA, the Medicaid Community Attendant Services and Supports Act , which would allow eligible individuals to spend their Medicaid allotment on attendant care in their homes.

ADAPT frequently converges on Washington, D.C., with the message: "Our Homes, Not Nursing Homes!"

Revolving door: inaccessible to people who use wheelchairs. Wheelchair in a revolving door: inaccessible to everyone.

"You are the true patriots." -Justin Dart

Sermon at Chestnut Hill United Methodist Chruch - 8/25/96

The Rev. Nellie Greene

Good morning. This reading is from the Gospel of Matthew, 15:21-28

21 Leaving that place, Jesus withdrew to the region of Tyre and Sidon. 22 A Canaanite woman from that vicinity came to him, crying out, "Lord, Son of David, have mercy on me! My daughter is suffering terribly from demon possession." 23 Jesus did not answer a word. So his disciples came to him and urged him, "Send her away, for she keeps crying out after us." 24 He answered, "I was sent only to the lost sheep of Israel." 25 The woman came and knelt before him. "Lord, help me!" she said. 26 He replied, "It is not right to take the children's bread and toss it to their dogs." 27 "Yes, Lord," she said, "but even the dogs eat the crumbs that fall from their masters' table." 28 Then Jesus answered, "Woman, you have great faith! Your request is granted." And her daughter was healed from that very hour, for God's gifts and his call are irrevocable.

In the name of God: our Creator, Redeemer, and Friend along the way. Amen.

Good morning. This is a very challenging reading, and let me set the scene. We have a woman, who is clearly an outsider, turning to Jesus for help, and he doesn't appear to be receptive. Nor do his disciples. They are annoyed, because she is making such a nuisance of herself. She trails after

Jesus, crying for mercy, pleading with him to heal her daughter, who has some sort of schizophrenia, and she won't take no for an answer. Apparently, she traveled quite a distance to see Jesus, and she would not let him off the hook. She is probably very scared, but she is also desperate, knowing this chance may never come again. She gathers her courage together, and simply goes for it. This must have been a pretty lonely mission.

"Send this woman away!" say the disciples. She is driving everybody crazy. Jesus reluctantly agrees to speak to her, and when he does, he not only points out she's a foreigner, but he insults her. He practically calls her a dog. Even so, this woman persists. She humbles herself, and says she'd be grateful for even a crumb. Her response to Jesus is remarkable, and he is apparently so moved by her persistence and faith in his power, he grants her request. He respects her, even though she is different.

What I've learned from this reading is this woman had a dream, and was willing to pursue it until she achieved it. She was ostracized, but she did not give up. She turned to the only one person around who she thought could help her, and this was Jesus. Her act showed extraordinary courage and faith. I'm not sure why Jesus wasn't interested in helping her at first. The text implies he was concerned because she was a foreigner, but maybe he was just having a bad day.

There is another woman whom I know, who was also an outsider with a dream, and she wouldn't let God off the hook until she had achieved it. Like the woman in this story, this woman was clearly an outsider who faced many obstacles. She was never ostracized to the same extent, but many people told her she was a fool, and others actively discouraged her.

Her dream was to go to a college, which was a 7 hour drive away from home, to get her degree, and graduate in the usual 4 years. The only trouble was, this woman could barely walk and talk, and she couldn't write with a pen or a pencil, and she was too blind to read. But, like I've said, she was pretty determined.

Like the Canaanite woman, this woman was pretty scared when she got to this College, and like the Canaanite woman, hers was a lonely mission. She had to get up at 5:00 every morning, because it took her 3-4 hours to shower and dress for her morning classes. When a friend she made there noticed she was skipping breakfast, he offered to bring her some on his way to class, so for a couple of years at least, she subsisted in the morning on an amazing liquid concoction of brewers yeast, granola and yogurt, along with a glass of orange juice, a cup of coffee, and a donut.

She was too proud to use a wheelchair, or other assisting device, so when she stumbled on the ice while on her way to the dining commons or to class, she got on her knees and crawled, until she reached where she was headed. Usually though, there were plenty of other students around to help her reach her various destinations safely.

Because she couldn't write, she was very observant in class, and somehow cajoled the smartest students into sharing their notes with her, and helping her prepare for mutual tests. But this

College had a remarkable examination system, which enabled her to learn, study, and progress without too many unnecessary complications. Technology hadn't advanced as far as it has today, so instead of a computer, she had to rely on a funky, large print, electric typewriter to communicate with her friends and professors. She was never completely sure if what she had typed was written correctly, and had some hilarious sessions deciphering her spelling with the various people whom she hired to retype her papers. Her pockets always held variously color coded index cards with oddly spelled words, which asked questions, and expressed her needs.

She had to learn everything through listening, and this was a novel experience, because previously she had been quite a talker. Her books from the Library for the Blind came on big reel to reel tapes, and being rather uncoordinated, it was a tremendous feat for this woman to read them. Sometimes she'd drop a reel on the floor, and watch in utter horror as it rolled along the carpet. When this happened, she wanted to cry and simply yell! But she managed to contain herself. If it was too late at night to seek help from a floor-mate, or if no one was around, she got down on the floor, and in considerable pain, she carefully rewound that darn reel, thanking her lucky stars she could see as well as she did. When her mother started reading some of her books to her, and mailing her the tapes on cassette, it was an incredible relief.

It took her an entire day to do her laundry, and when a floor-mate discovered her battling with quarters in the basement laundry one weekend, he not only helped her insert the blasted coins in the machine, but graciously offered to do her wash whenever he did his. Nothing was easy for her. Still this woman doggedly persisted. Like the woman in today's reading, she knew this chance might never come again, and like the woman in today's reading, this woman didn't feel any great encouragement from God. Instead, she felt God challenging her and questioning her motives. Most of the time, she was simply too exhausted to give God much thought, and when she did pray, it was to beg God to get her through another day.

In reflecting about this college experience, I realize that Jesus was with her every step of the way. Even when she didn't feel his presence, he was there. He came to her in the person of wonderful professors, who bent over backwards to help her achieve. He came to her in the form of many friends who read to her, studied with her, ate with her, and just plain laughed and had fun with her. He came to her in the form of a girlfriend, who drove her to church some Sundays, on the back of her motorcycle. He came to her through the friends who did her laundry and made sure she ate properly, and he came to her in the really beautiful New England landscape.

Another critical lesson we can learn from this text is that God hears us when we cry out. Even when we think God is ignoring us, God is really there. Remember that Jesus did not pay attention to his disciples when they told him to send this Canaanite woman away. Instead, he met with her and heard her out. Granted, he challenged her purpose by asking her some tough questions, but if our motives are honest and just, we must never feel afraid to turn to God. In case you haven't guessed by now, this woman was me.

The thought I will close with is no matter how much we might feel like outsiders, this passage demonstrates that all of us belong. Never forget this!

Come, let us pray:

Good and loving God, we thank you for confronting us with this demanding passage, and we thank you for this church. We thank you for coming to us in the person of our friends and neighbors. We thank you for challenging us, and asking us tough questions. We thank you for giving us Jesus.

Please show us you hear us when we cry for mercy, and give us the courage and will to persevere when we face trouble and difficulty, and show us how to love each other, and respect our differences. In your name we pray. Amen.

Why be an Activist

Maria Dewan

Some may question the relevance of activism and involvement in a political movement. Others may think those who are active are a bunch of greasy-haired troublemakers who have nothing better to do with their time. With all this negativity, we have to ask ourselves, "Is it worthwhile attending protest marches and rallies? What does it really accomplish?" I argue that participating in advocacy and activism in support of disability rights is extremely important for many different reasons.

Education can be considered the primary goal of activism. Unfortunately, we live in a world where disabilities are not understood, or are ignored altogether. To overcome this, we must make our needs known to government officials and other powerful figures. When we do this, we educate society in general on the obstacles we face as people with disabilities.

Through education, we hope influential people will acknowledge us and bring forth changes to policies, or make new ones which will improve our lives. This may be the most important reason people become activists – to make life better for themselves and for the ones they love.

In the Spring of 2000, a group of disability rights advocates, myself included, went to Washington, D.C. for a press conference to reintroduce MiCASSA by Senators Specter and Harkin. MiCASSA is the latest version of a national attendant care bill that would give persons with disabilities options other than living in nursing homes. Our strong presence at that press conference demonstrated our true desire to make MiCASSA a reality. Any legislator or member of the media there that day could see it.

Empowerment is another advantage of activism. When someone is discouraged about a situation like transportation or housing, he may think, "What can I do about it?" However, when he joins with others to fight for change, and then witnesses the change happen, that same person will feel powerful and say, "Yes, there is something I can do about it!" People working together are the key to empowerment and successful activism.

In the past, the ADA has been challenged, and its future placed in jeopardy. When this happens, advocates from across our country gather in Washington, D.C., for marches and rallies to support this law. Those who participate in these activities are powerful because together we are standing up for our rights. We are a force that will not be denied, and the ADA is alive and well because of it.

The personal enrichment an advocate gains through traveling is something that cannot be underestimated. Think of someone who was institutionalized and then gets connected with an organization like ADAPT. This person now has the chance to visit cities in other parts of the country where he or she has never been. This opportunity to travel would have never existed if it weren't for his or her involvement in activism.

Personally, I've been to Washington, D.C., and

Harrisburg numerous times for conferences, rallies and other activities. I have been in the offices of federal and state congressmen and I have even shaken hands with former U.S. Attorney General Janet Reno. These have all been tremendous experiences for me with memories to last a lifetime.

There is also a sense of community that goes along with being an activist, especially at the state level. Whenever I'm in Harrisburg for a protest or an Independent Living conference, I always recognize faces that are familiar from other events. We get to know each other, thus forming our own subculture.

Being part of a group such as the disability rights movement can eliminate feelings of isolation that are often experienced because of disability. Friendships are formed or renewed whenever advocates unite. These friendships can blossom into something more meaningful long after the advocacy is finished. Therefore, socialization is one of the best benefits associated with activism. This is particularly true for people with disabilities who at times have difficulty gaining acceptance from family and other non-disabled peers.

It is clear that activism has a vital place in the disability culture. To those who are participants — keep up the good work. There is still a lot to be done. For those who are thinking about joining the movement — I urge you to do so. Not only will you be making a positive change in the world, but the other rewards you will receive will exceed your expectations.

The Malingerer Goes to the Movies

for Colin Kempner and Judith Wright

Scott Norman

1

You're sitting there, and it's getting harder to
  breathe.
It seems as if a tiny man, like a gnome,
has crept up the back of the seat, and dropped a
  net,
into your head, over your brain . . .
You glance at the woman sitting next to you,
and she doesn't look like she's there . . .
You look at the screen and it seems unreal,
like a bad film.

2

Are you in a theater at all?
Are you in a room filled with water?
ARE THERE ANY PEOPLE HERE?!

3

The show's over, you're out in the parking lot,
wondering how to get home . . .

Signs of Protest

Jessie Jane Lewis

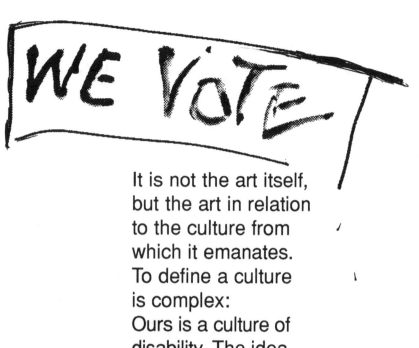

It is not the art itself,
but the art in relation
to the culture from
which it emanates.
To define a culture
is complex:
Ours is a culture of
disability. The idea
is not to give the
answers but to pose
the questions.

The stakes are higher. I can't afford to waste time making art. I paint protest signs. Signs that say **"LET ME IN"**, **"EQUAL ACCESS NOW"**, **"HEALTH-CARE FOR ALL"**, **"GIVE ME LITERACY or GIVE ME DEATH "** Trying to understand the situation through art. This type of work is important because it gives the able bodied population a glimpse of a world that anyone could someday inhabit. At last, I am in the right place at the right time. In this culture of disability, the message takes precedence over the medium.

**If I could walk,
where would I go?
My destination
would be the same.**

Don't get caught short.
Love is blind.
Sitting around on my
fat ass.
Dumb and Dumber.
Roll with the punches.
Stand up for your rights.
Walk don't run.
Fall on deaf ears.
Hot to trot.

As we talk to each other and discuss issues and strategies, we begin to define ourselves as a community. This defining process begins within our ranks, not from some outside source. We have to know who we are first before we can present our ideas to the outside world.

Before I was disabled, I worked in a nursing home. I was a recreation therapist. What a joke, but that's another story. They had one large, white tiled room for the showers. If pressed for time, the aides showered the men and women together in that room separated by a curtain down the center but really you could see around it. There was one woman whom the aides called "Gummy" because she had no teeth. Also she was a screamer. When they turned the shower hose on her, well, she was confused, but she knew enough to scream in terror.

Performance by people with disabilities? It's a natural. Disability is spectacle. It is street theater. Everywhere I go people stare at my legs. And it is hard for a disabled person to sneak in late to a meeting, for example. We are forced to make an entrance. Aren't the recent civil actions by people with disabilities simply performance pieces in disguise?

If you are disabled, it doesn't necessarily mean you are in poor health. And if you are sick, it doesn't necessarily mean you are disabled.

LIMITATION would be a good title for an art exhibit and symposia that would explore taboo subjects relating to disability: sex and the cripple, anger and the law, incontinence, the general public's preconceptions about disability and inability. The project could be an investigation into how the body is capable of making art.
And how each one of us has the potential for embarrassing ourselves either through a physical or mental infirmity or through a politically incorrect pronouncement.

How does art take shape within the community and become a genre? The idea of LIMITATION is a point of departure for the making of art.

Able bodied people are afraid to offend the disabled person. They don't know what to say to us. How to "help". What a privilege it is to help someone. How dare anyone presume how to help a disabled person or even whether they need helping. A project would be to explore these ideas of "helping".

Limitation = Humanity = Art

Last year I worked on a skilled floor of a small community hospital. Most of my patients were recently disabled. I guess you could say I was on both sides of the treatment divide. When people go through a physical challenge to their system, it often leads to a change in how they view themselves and how they spend their time. The reverse is also true: When people stop doing the things they love or when there is a change in routine or role, their health declines.

BODY plus MIND equals INTELLIGENCE

I smudge the boundaries between different media. **All** of my work documents the journey of **my body** through disability. The images exploit **my vulnerability** and dealings with limitations **and barriers.** **I grieve** for the past as revealed in **choice** of subject: a ruined building, a checkered **past** in which I ran and swam freely, and **thoughts** of the food in French. I became part of **a minority** any of us can join in an instant and **I plunder** this rich field for images and statements.

My art refers to physical decline and the required treatments. I document my own and other people's stories. In a past video work, Stings, (1993), I documented painful and pleasurable treatments with bee venom therapy to treat bladder incontinence. Sometimes feeling pain is better than feeling nothing at all. And any of us, even the able bodied, can be numb.

As patient and therapist, we would

embark on discussion. I sometimes

drew their portrait. The portrait can

be the tool that facilitates the therapy.

Sometimes the very act of sitting still

for 10 minutes was a goal in itself

and I had to work very quickly with

very few strokes. My hands were

sometimes shaky so the act was a

challenge to me as well. People's

mental and emotional state is tied up

with the physical and it shows up in

the portrait.

One time, I was going to a presentation about funding for the arts. The presentation was held on the second floor of an inaccessible building, and it was raining out. I was so mad, especially because it was a state program, and I couldn't get in. Later, I wrote a complaint letter to that organization and got a very curious response. I received a phone call at my studio from the woman in charge. She said, "You should have banged on the front door and asked for me." She was sure that they would have gladly interrupted the program to accommodate me. She said she would've been happy to come out to the sidewalk to give me a special presentation. "In the rain?" I asked. (It was a two-hour presentation) She reconsidered. "They would carry you up the stairs in your wheelchair." she said. I was angry and forget what my response was, but I think I hung up. The whole thing felt like discrimination. The law says "No discrimination allowed". They should have carried <u>everyone</u> up, then it would not have been discrimination; It would have been a performance piece .

Once I met Linda Montano, the famous performance artist, and I am proud to say she authorized purchase of some of my video works by the University of Texas at Austin. She said, "You are the lucky one. You get to change peoples' thinking." Truthfully, I don't know what I'm doing. I'm flying blind. But someone just gave me a fully accessible van with hand controls and a ramp. So maybe this time I'm on the right track.

It's not how you walk but where you stand.

It is impossible for someone who is not disabled to understand. We refuse to allow others to think they can empower us. We empower ourselves. Registering to vote and going to the polls is vital to getting the legislators to address our issues. We will get quality health care, adequate education, full employment, accessible public transportation, housing, access to the arts, and more, when we register in large numbers and vote in each election. Then, and only then, will the politicians see us as a voting bloc.

Learn the wheelchair.

A person can get by
using their disability
for only so long.
Sooner or later you got
to show the moxie.

If you are going to be disabled, you had better be rich.

I'm going places most people never visit.

Sometimes I would like
to remain anonymous,
but can't.

I have no privacy; my
disability is evident to
all.

to explore the frame around the art is like looking at the chair a person sits in.

A New Disability Manifesto

Josie Byzek

Nonviolent resistance ... is based on the conviction that the universe is on the side of justice. Consequently, the believer in nonviolence has deep faith in the future.

—Martin Luther King, Jr.

Everyone is a jerk, according to many in Pennsylvania's disability movement, unless our leadership says that they are OK. Most people — especially nondisabled people — are out to make money off of us, kill us, sweep us out of the way, or take care of us in such a patronizing fashion that they choke the life out of us. Therefore, we must fight back, and the best way to fight back is to find leaders who will help us plug into our anger and spew it out on anyone who disagrees with us. We must give these leaders 100 percent unquestionable support.

Many leaders in our movement will tell you this philosophy is based on truly great leaders such as Mahatma Gandhi and Martin Luther King, Jr. But neither Gandhi nor King ever even insinuated that the societal institutions oppressing their people were in place because most whites were unwilling to end the oppression of nonwhites. In fact, both men believed that most people — even white people — are basically moral. Once they clearly saw the injustices they were party to –

showcased by acts of civil disobedience, if necessary — they would insist the injustice end, and would even willingly give up some of their own societal privileges. This belief in the basic goodness of India's oppressors is how Gandhi was able to convince the powerful British empire to loosen its grip on India and Pakistan. This belief in the inevitable victory of justice in the hearts of humanity is how King garnered, eventually, the support of the white President and white Attorney General to take a stand against segregation. Neither India nor America would have willingly let go of their unjust policies if either of these men operated from the philosophy that most whites are not moral people. If that were so, why waste time trying to change and challenge their hearts?

And hear this loud and clear: neither of these men could have achieved the victories they did if their own communities did not constantly hold them accountable for their actions.

Unfortunately, many leaders in the disability community operate under a much different assumption than either Gandhi or King. They do not believe the larger, nondisabled, community will change their attitudes or policies dealing with disability unless disabled people force them to change against their will. Invite them to ally with us? Never. We can't trust them.

But then, maybe our leaders' disbelief in the inherent goodness of nondisabled people does not matter much, considering how quickly we consume our leaders with our twisted concept of support. We do not question them enough; we do not hold them accountable for their thoughts, actions, or expenditures until it's too late. We mindlessly back them 100 percent, until they are so power-drunk and fiscally irresponsible that we have to take them out and replace them with new leaders that we will support 100 percent. And so it goes. No one, no matter how great a leader he or she may be, can handle the type of power we push on our leaders.

We are on the cusp of becoming a truly powerful international movement. To move over this cusp with grace and momentum, we must realign our philosophy and leadership goals with the movements we claim to emulate.

First, our goal for the wider community must be to invite them in as partners and allies with us. The oppression we are under is so obvious that once we point it out they will be won over, and will help us win our freedom. For example, when we must engage in civil disobedience, it should be with the goal of recruiting the people on the sidewalks to side with us. That means we have to stop using obscenities, stop insulting, slurring, or thinking the worst of people just because they are nondisabled.

Second, our goal within our own community must be to constantly recruit and cultivate new leadership, and to simultaneously hold our long-standing leaders accountable both fiscally and philosophically. The leaders we love the most ought to be the ones we question the most. Too many potentially great leaders in our state have shriveled on the vine because they thought they were above reproach. Some have made horrible errors of judgment that led to their disempowerment. They thought they were above reproach because we told them they were.

We don't have to lose any more potential allies or any more potentially great leaders. But we will lose them, unless we drastically adjust our philosophy to more accurately reflect the philosophies of the movements we claim to admire.

Disability Culture:
A Personal Experience

Sieglinde A. Shapiro

My introduction to disability culture began when I entered Widener Memorial School for Crippled Children. That segregated environment, which was created by mostly non-disabled professionals, affected me indelibly. It brought together those of us who would have otherwise been isolated, and it instilled among us the resolve to change the system that kept us separate. Despite its negative intent, it was an incubator of disability culture.

Mimi Nelken and I attended Widener together. Years later, in 1973, it was Mimi who told me about Judy Heumann and Disabled in Action of New York. Judy and I had experienced the same kind of discrimination, having been denied teaching positions due to our disabilities. However, my protests to the Philadelphia School Board were unproductive, while Judy sued the NYC schools and won. DIA was born of that battle and now Mimi was asking me if I wanted to bring DIA to Pennsylvania. Realizing the potential for change, I agreed.

1973 saw the Disability Rights movement explode. While some parents and professionals had gotten a few laws enacted, including Section 504 of the 1973 Rehabilitation Act, and some groups provided services, relatively few disabled people had previously been directly involved as advocates.

That year saw the creation of many so-called consumer groups. Having witnessed other civil rights activities, we realized that being disabled and treated as "special" people was not special. Indeed, going to separate "special" schools, living in segregated institutions, and attending "special" camps and recreational programs really fostered our exclusion. We recognized that the environment was inaccessible and excluded us from the mainstream. Perhaps worst of all, American public policy codified certain prejudices and reinforced our segregation from the mainstream.

DIA of Pennsylvania first met in June of 1973. We identified specific concerns and began a media campaign to alert the public and build our membership. We spoke to any group that would listen, and helped produce a groundbreaking TV-10 series called "Making It: the Able Disabled." It won many awards and put DIA on the map.

Our first campaigns targeted employment discrimination and inaccessible public transportation. Our first great victory was amending the Human Relations Act to ban employment discrimination against Pennsylvanians with disabilities. We were joined by other consumer groups like Operation Overcome, Open Doors, the PA Council of the Blind, and the PA Society for Advancement of the Deaf. Together we later founded the PA Alliance of the Physically Handicapped (PAPH), which became PCCD, the PA Coalition of People with Disabilities, in 1982.

Local and statewide coalitions soon became a national movement. In 1976, we joined sister DIA groups in New York, New Jersey and Baltimore, the Paralyzed Veterans of America (PVA) and 7 others to sue the U.S. Secretary of Transportation, demanding access to all mass transit buses. The TRANSBUS suit, or *DIA of PA et. al. v. Coleman*, brought together 12 million disabled, elderly and minority Americans to fight for this right.

Americans with disabilities were also waiting for 504 regulations to be issued and nothing was happening. When the administration changed in Washington in 1977, we would wait no more. That April, the new American Coalition of Citizens with Disabilities (ACCD) asked DIA of PA to organize a demonstration and meeting with the heads of Region III's Office for Civil Rights (OCR) in the U.S. Department of Health, Education and Welfare (HEW) demanding immediate promulgation of 504 regulations. Nine other regions also demonstrated. Philadelphia achieved its goal, getting OCR to Telex a joint demand to Secretary Califano.

A few very active years had forged much unity and a stronger disability community, making 1977 a significant year. First, we secured the "TRANSBUS Mandate" requiring all new mass transit buses be equipped with a low floor, a wide door and a ramp. Next, our 504 demonstrations culminated in the issuance of regulations. And finally, President Carter announced an Independent Living office in HUD at the first and only White House Conference on Handicapped Individuals.

However, I believe that the most important outcome was the training of more disabled leaders through subsequent "504 Workshops," creating more advocates who would join our movement. Consequently, the 80's saw passage of many disability rights: a Fair Housing Act amendment banning discrimination; the Elderly and Handicapped Voting Act of 1982 requiring equal access for federal elections; the Air Carrier Access Act of 1986, prohibiting discrimination by airlines; and 1988's "Tech Act" supporting assistive technology.

We didn't win equal access to public transportation during this time. Unfortunately, our lawsuit was declared moot when the TRANSBUS mandate was issued. We thought that we'd won, but soon learned that policies can be circumvented by those determined to do so. The Southeastern PA Transit Authority (SEPTA) and two other transit authorities had agreed to order TRANSBUS but all three U.S. bus manufacturers refused to retool and build accessible buses. It took the ADA to finally resolve the issue. In 1978 ACCD called a transportation summit meeting in Denver and ADAPT (Americans Disabled for Accessible Public Transportation) took over the battle. They led the way to the current provisions under Title II of the ADA.

A decade of activism had taught us that our strength depends on a cross-disability perspective. In 1982, PCCD focused its advocacy efforts on securing "attendant care," or Personal Assistance Services (PAS), for all People with Disabilities. DIA of PA and five other consumer groups organized Centers for Independent Living (CILs) throughout the state, and joined PCCD to advocate for statewide PAS. We conducted advocacy training, published an advocacy manual that became the blueprint for other states, established a Harrisburg office and visited the General Assembly often. Finally, the Attendant Care Act of 1986 was enacted. Over $150 million has since been allocated for PAS programs.

Advocating for the ADA also kept us busy. This effort in particular allowed us to learn more about our peers from other disability groups and their particular experiences. All of this coalition building led to a disability culture enhanced by diversity and interaction.

It has been 29 years since Mimi and I became disability rights activists. During those years I have made many friends and learned several important lessons. I urge my readers to take heart and take these lessons to heart. First, the disability rights movement was born out of common experiences of discrimination, which caused our segregation in education and social activities; inferior training and work opportunities; and an infrastructure excluding us from "normal" daily activities.

Our common history also includes the eugenics movement led by Social Darwinists, advocating genocide, the prohibition of marriage, and sterilization for certain People with Disabilities. Through all this we have developed our own culture, with our own values, games, beliefs, languages, groups and support systems. We can be proud of our culture and our accomplishments.

We who became disabled during the developmental years or through aging have experienced these phenomena acutely because we've been segregated in "special" schools, service programs, workshops, and nursing homes. However, prejudice and segregation remain the predominant response to disability by American society.

Even as we continue fighting for integration and inclusion, let's not forget that those settings also provided some positive outcomes. Even as we struggle for total integration of our people, we must not neglect our particular culture, Disability Culture, which holds us together. It is a powerful culture, one in which just a few people can alter mighty systems.

We must learn our history, remember its lessons and practice peer support. While continuing to advocate for integration and inclusion, we must acknowledge our responsibility to share our wisdom with young and old, disabled and non-disabled, allies and friends. We must support and nurture our disabled peers, our families and allies because it is our past, our continued cultural development, our collective action and peer support which are the keys to our future.

Selections from
Transcendent Visions

Introduction by David Kime, Editor

Transcendent Visions was born in the summer of 1992. I found the first issue to be vile and obnoxious, so I threw out all the copies I had left and sent apology letters to all the folks in the mental health movement that I had initially sent it to. When I was hospitalized for depression, I received several letters from supportive people who told me what a great idea it was for me to start a low budget literary magazine written by people who have been in the mental health system. One letter said, "We need a place to rant against the system."

Today, *Transcendent Visions* is about to celebrate ten years of publishing. I am very proud of some of the work that has appeared, and I am glad that I am giving a voice to folks who are often stigmatized by society. Being an artistic person recovering from a mental illness, I feel it is vital for us to speak out against all the negativity in a positive and articulate fashion. Art shows us in a different light and helps strip us of our labels.

I try to tell people who write me that they are not a "schizophrenic" or a "bipolar," they are human beings. I have found many of them to harbor a great deal of internalized stigma. This means that they began to believe all the junk society has thrown at us. One brilliantly creative individual wrote me and said, "I have become used to being viewed as subhuman since I am schizophrenic." I wrote him back and tried to stress how we are human beings who have a lot to share with the world.

Throughout history, people with mental illness have contributed greatly to our society, both politically and culturally. Winston Churchill often wrote and spoke about his depression. Vincent Van Gogh acknowledged his severe ups and downs in his letters to his brother, Theo. Unfortunately, our society turns a blind eye to what we have contributed as people and brands us with hurtful negative labels like "psycho," "lunatic," or "crazy."

I truly believe that people are born with a predisposition towards mental illness, and then environmental stresses bring these conditions out. I also feel that medication is a necessity for me if I want to live a somewhat symptom-free life. (I refuse to use the word "normal," since it implies boring and unimaginative.) But others do not agree with this viewpoint, and I often print their views despite my disagreement. In a recent issue of my political zine, *Crazed Nation*, I printed an article in which the writer stressed how running vigorously five times a week has cured him of his depression. In another issue I printed a letter in which the writer spoke out against antipsychotic medications, siding with the writings of Peter Breggin. In his book *Toxic Psychiatry*, Breggin stresses the harmful effects of these drugs, citing conditions like tardive dyskinesia, a painful twitching resulting from many years or decades of antipsychotic usage.

We need open dialogue to grow as people. Our needs must be met by the mental health system, and we must be respected by society. We need to stop forced treatment, restraints, and close all those state hospitals. They are nothing more than human warehouses. We need to be reintegrated into society, and to seek meaningful employment, not some job at a local fast food establishment. We need to speak out for ourselves, and demand equal rights instead of letting mental health professionals and groups like the National Alliance of the Mentally Ill speak for us. Respect for us will come through our becoming vocal and presenting our side of the story in an articulate and respectful manner. It is time for our voices to be heard, but lashing out against others only causes more stigma, since it perpetuates the negative image. It is this positive image that I am trying to provide through *Transcendent Visions* and *Crazed Nation.*

Kime

70

Editor's Note: The following pages have been selected from the remarkable ten-year run of *Transcendent Visions*; what is reproduced here is barely a fraction of that which was originally published. In transferring this work from the 'zine to book format, an effort has been made to preserve the informality and immediacy inherent in the original photocopied product.

Selections from
Transcendent Visions: 1992 - 2001

TRANSCENDENT VISIONS FALL 1998

NO RESTRAINTS

Greg Wyatt, cover for *Transcendent Visions*, Fall, 1999.

Car On Fire   by Beth Greenspan

Poisonous smoke cloud
Chases me up the street
During morning traffic.
Chases me up the street
Cornering me in a doorway,
Trying to seep into my eyes,
My thoughts of survival.
I try to run in the direction
I need to go, where the cloud
Cannot follow.
I get across the street,
And become one with the sidewalk,
Pavement dreams.
I become the bitter blue wind,
The snow trying to permeate
Deep into the core of the Earth,
Core of the Earth that is now me.
I no longer have a use for walking.
I float down the supposed street,
Poisonous smoke cloud
Giving chase, sneaking in through my ears,
And some of the blackness
Started sinking into my open membranes.
When I reach where I'm going,
I sit on a couch
Trying to exhale.
Breathe, breathe, breathe
And don't fall down.
I make a run for the next world,
But I get shoved back onto the sofa cushion,
Smell of poisonous smoke cloud
Drifts through as a flashback,
Chasing me down to the ground,
Body shaking, swaying,
Like a chorus of wind-ripped trees
In bitter blue wind.

A Book of Revelations   by Alan Catlin

Writing things down meant
saving all the silver wrapper
inserts that cigarettes came in.
That they contained smoke meant
the paper was magical and all
things magical were sacred.
What she wrote down was from a new
Bible transmitted from a radio
tower in New York City that only
an amanuensis could write down.
It was a long book of revelations
that could not be saved that was
slowly being covered by tidal changes.
She could see it all from her window
from the sixth floor; Manhattan
was the last refuge. I wanted
to ask her where the cigarettes
came from after hearing that:
"The Confederate South is all covered
by water. None of these states have
actually existed for almost one hundred
years." All the cartons of cigarettes
she had stored away under the bed
came from North Carolina; that was
a place for her that didn't exist.
Looking out her window after she died
of cancer I saw an antediluvian world
through a nicotine nightmare of stained
glass I wished had never existed.

Drawing
by Robert Bullock

What She Said   by Ann A. Boger

Never mind the steel door,
it's for your protection.
Send those rings home,
you never know around here.
Don't worry about her cries,
you'll get used to them.
Seventy-two hours,
then we'll see.
Wear street clothes,
we want you to feel normal.
I'm sorry, but I'll have to take
these make-up bottles to the desk.
Now in your own words,
tell me tell me tell.
There are no locks on doors,
no bathtubs, no mirrors.
Let me see those wrists,
tsk, tsk, ugly business, girl.
Hair dryers not allowed in rooms,
no belts either.
You're on thirty-minute checks,
you'll see a lot of me.
What? Lord, Lord
what is that doctor thinking
releasing you so soon!
You'll be back,
ones like you always are.

Transcendent visions
Summer 1997. Celebrating
Five years of madness.

Cover art by Greg Wyatt

Two poems from the Frank series   by CA Conrad

Frank was embarrassed in the bar
when his skin began to smoke again

"hey man!" someone yelled
"do you need the fire department?"

everybody laughed

"No" he said with a nervous smile
waving his arm to clear the smoke
which only made it worse
"it will pass" he said
"it's just the condition of my soul

it will pass"

Drawing by Jason McLean

Frank and his wife
sat at the dinner table

baked and glazed
the ham stood from the platter
demanded prayer
clean hands
kind speech in his honor

"DON'T LOOK AT MY LIFE FROM
THE CORNER OF YOUR EYE!" the ham hollered

they begged forgiveness
and honored his request

the ham grunted
as their knives pulled him apart
he wiggled and smoothed out
sighing on their tongues

Frank kissed the naked bone
over and over
held it to the sunlight kissing it

the bone purred all night
from the foot of the bed.

The Day The World Went Nuts   by Joe Randell

I woke up one day and everything had changed. Though I was unconscious of the change, I now wonder why it wasn't obvious to me at the time.

I turned on the radio and the DJ was talking about his tenth grade math teacher. Then he talked about domestic chores at his household . . . how his wife earned more money than him . . . how hard it was just to read a book with three kids jumping around the house. He then said: "This song is the most inane piece of bullshit I've ever heard!" and put on some music.

"Wow!" I wondered aloud, "I've never heard anything like that on the radio!" And then I said, "Maybe this guy is cracking up? Maybe the guys in the white coats are taking him away right now? Hmm . . ." I mused, "if I wear this black T-shirt people will think I have a death obsession. Well, I do, don't I? Oh to hell with it — I'll wear something else."

I fixed my breakfast carrying on a monologue with the refrigerator, fry pan and my canaries about topics past, future concerns and speculations . . . But most discomforting was my oratory on the present. I began asking questions — lots of them — and answering them with a rock-solid certainty, with nobody for an audience except for my canaries. "Well, glad to see you're pleased!" I said to them and walked outside and up the steps to the street. On the way up the steps I passed a woman who was muttering something about tampons and foreplay. I gave her a military salute and said – "May the force be with you today, madam!" Proceeding onward, I said aloud "I'll have to see about her later!"

Walking through town everybody was talking. The place was a gushing river of consciousness. Anything was said whenever and wherever people pleased, whether to other persons or empty space. I saw one sight that made me laugh. A punk skateboarder kid telling a cop to jam something up his ass. The cop, with a look of deep concentration in his eyes, explained to the young man the anatomical improbability of such an event occurring. The boy said to himself as the cop walked away, "There are many things in this life I do not understand," and went over to talk to some young woman sitting on a bench.

I walked along toward the public library chattering like a maniac. Everybody else was doing the same. I walked into the library and the place was roaring with spoken words. Some were laughing uncontrollably, others had tears rolling down their cheeks. One man in his late 50s was pounding his fist on the counter at the librarian's station, raging on about something that happened 150 years ago, while the librarian sat there in rapt attention, eating a bowl of chocolate ice cream.

Then someone or something brushed up against my back. I fell to the floor. Blacked out.

I awoke strapped to a bed in the seclusion room at St. Joseph's psychiatric ward. A doctor came in. He reassured me that I'd be well soon, that in the future things would be fine if I only stuck with my medication regimen. As he walked toward the door, I heard him say, "If Nancy is cheating on me . . . . should we see a marriage counselor, or what?!" As I lay there strapped to that bed, I listened to his laughter as he walked down the hall.

P.M.   by B. Z. Niditch

The clever talk
covers up
rumor, gossip, politics
of the short sleeved
and mini skirted
presumably demanding
a drink, a kiss, a joke
on this happy hour
with the sense of freedom
of a news-less time
when work is extinct
as the toy dinosaur at FAO's
where the pretty children
stare on the edge
of a prelapsarian hour
and townsfolk make their way
by train to suburban bliss
passing each other's notice
but oblivious of their lives.

The evening papers rattle on
about the latest rumor of war
the earliest city murder
but nothing can stop it
not even the last train
out to the kiosks
of the world
in crowded subways
crossing heartless bridges
midway between the traffic
of flesh and love object,
the handlebars of fantasies
between heels, knees and pants
wishing to be in bed

drunk with conquests
for a testy, fast mover
in a no-question-asked night
that the day accomplished
in its monosyllabic chatter
the fragility of obsessions
confidence in our imperfection,
wishing that Miss Anxiety
would cool you off
and Mr. Temper
could vanish in changed skin
as you relinquish your horizon
of trousers, shirt and underwear
submerging your dream
despite the night's fixity
of blitzkrieg panic attacks,
your mind already racing
for the next A.M.

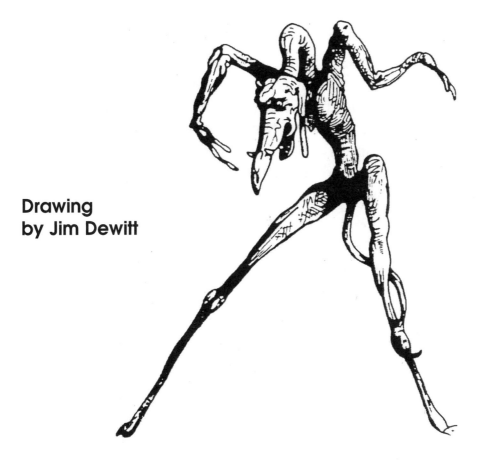

**Drawing
by Jim Dewitt**

CHEMICAL WARFARE   by Bonnie Henderson Schell

I let out the dog, and as my feet pads meet the
        walnut
inlaid floor, the smell begins.
Sweet seeping wires, burning through my cells.
It follows me down the hall,
surrounds me while I sit to urinate, rising with me,
as I flush a doughnut of mist around my neck,
pulling me forward.
Petite. Small in that no one else smells it.
I watch the dog coming in. Large
enough to halt my plans.
Mal. Malevolent. No use to look for its source
in appliances, shorted-out, dead flowers, spilled
bottles in the cabinets. It hides.
My Creator's secret weapon. I am unemployed.
White manic female volunteer.

There is no patriot missile for my protection.
Yesterday I dwelled in a state of peace,
but overnight, I surmised the rebellion on the
        borders.
In the past I might tiptoe away from it, adopting
shallow breathing, sleep, a frozen stance,
digging in and down for the coming slaughter . . .
I breathe deeply. Now reckless, daring.
I stomp forward in my combat hightops,
exhaling with defiance.
Bite the smell and chew it.

Transcendent Visions Summer 1996

Cover art by Greg Wyatt, 1996.

Always   by Chriss-Spike Quatrone

"The abusers always seem to be around." –Doc

everywhere. Leaning over the bathtub
with her prying soapy hand.
Under the bedclothes in my scariest dream.
Tickling me while I watch cartoons
on t.v. until I scream
and force feeding me cod liver oil
after breakfast.

She's calling me bad names.
Telling me I'm dirty, filthy, stupid.
Claiming I didn't tell her where I went
and then yelling at me for it over the phone
but I knew I'd told her, and I'd bring
her a Christmas ornament from the school fair or
a slice of cold pizza, hoping it would shut her up.
Now she's dragging me across the rug
scarring my knees. Now she's throwing
me down the stairs. Now she's beating me
and punching me with an umbrella,
with her fists. And then later she bought
herself an expensive ring to comfort herself
after I left. Still later she wants me to say
that I had a happy childhood.

Art by Greg Wyatt

Dan Neubauer's "Mallory Will" is a regular feature
of *Transcendent Visions*.

Zyprexa zoned, Clonepin clobbered and Depakote delivered

Donnie Means

Psycho test tubed like after my lithium sunrises and lifts is how I feel sometimes. As my drug acclimations windows hadn't yet opened, yet my anxiety levels were tighter than a polypropylene knot!

Once again metaphysically I had a new drug regimen to adjust to. A whole new set of surprises, losses and gifts.

Zyprexa and Depakote make my life more manageable, more level, so I don't frighten everyone I come near. Clonepin can help me maintain my focus and decrease the agitation facilitated by anxiety attacks and racing thoughts of which can be inclined to be wrought.

In other words, the Zyprexa zap keeps me muzzled, while the Depakote delivery suppresses the lashing out erratically and irrationally at people uncontrollably.

Together these chemicals have made the difference between fear and freedom for me. I know for a fact that probably for the rest of my life I'll be taking some drug for the rest of my life to allow me to stay alive and/or co-exist. The thought frightened for a while.

Then another thought came over and that was that we live in no other time where bipolar or any other person deemed mentally wasn't victimized, institutionalized or quietly killed. I was spared all that along with many thousands of others.

So far as I'm concerned I'd rather be Zyprexa zapped and zoned, Clonepin clobbered and Depakote delivered than uncontrolled, dazed, delirious and in dubiously deadly flux. In the past people of my odd lot would've been killed, institutionalized, tortured or exorcised — imagine that!

Miss Mongolia and the Tree Ship
An excerpt, with illustrations by the author

Gabrielle R. Howee

Chapter 3: Captured!

Miss Mongolia's spacecraft had collided with something. She struggled to regain control of her ship. The barrier . . . of course. She must have run into the barrier that separates Mandal Earth from the rest of the solar system. Yes, in certain ages this barrier was in place to prevent Earthlings from using spaceships to go to other planets.

Miss Mongolia returned her attention to the ship's screen. There! In the distance there was a small island. Miss Mongolia steered her ship toward it. Hmmm. As Miss Mongolia closely flew over the island, she saw a landing circle and decided to land on it.

Miss Mongolia left her spacecraft to check her ship. Her ship was round and shaped like a cookie. Any damage could be easily seen. However, as Miss Mongolia stood in the opening of the hatch, she saw four men come out of the building which was close by. This building was close to the landing circle. Miss Mongolia had seen it from above, but she had assumed it was abandoned. In fact, the whole island had appeared to be uninhabited.

The four men from the building wore similar yellow clothing, and all were obesely fat. Compared to them, Miss Mongolia was as thin as a skeleton, and that is how they viewed her as she walked toward them. Very strange she seemed to them as she strode across the landing circle.

The hatch closed on her spacecraft, and she continued to walk toward the Earthlings. These fat men reminded Miss Mongolia of the larger Vramans of the priestly caste. Then, suddenly, Miss Mongolia was rushed and captured. Men had appeared from behind the four men, and had rushed her.

Miss Mongolia had cried out in surprise, but they did not let go. After dragging her into the building, the men strapped her down to a low rectangular bed. Then the door closed. She was left in the room alone.

ARA

ARA MEDITATING ON THE MOUNTAIN

Miss Mongolia lifted her head and stared at the ceiling. There was a small window in the room. Sunlight shone through the window and Miss Mongolia watched the rays of the sun play on the ceiling as the sun set. Then she closed her eyes and went to sleep.

Miss Mongolia awoke to find herself in a different room. There was a larger window in this room, and the morning sun was shining through it. Miss Mongolia looked down. She wasn't strapped down.

She sat up and looked around. There were two doors in the room. One probably led out; the other . . . . But then Miss Mongolia noticed the window. It was sealed. What type of place was this? Miss Mongolia got up to investigate the window. It was barred from opening from the inside and the outside. As the warm light from the rising sun fell on her face, Miss Mongolia gazed out of the window.

THE TOWERING WHITE BUILDING

AAIKA CHANGES TO MISS MONGOLIA

Where was she? Outside the large window she could see many trees, but the area seemed different from where she had landed. Had they moved her to a different place on the island?

Unknown to Miss Mongolia, the men who had taken her were part of a secret government section whose purpose was to design a way to break through the barrier which separated Earth from the other planets. To the higher authorities of the universe, such an endeavor would be considered insanity. Indeed, they would not approve. But the Earthlings had their plans, and would not be discouraged.

When the alien Miss Mongolia had walked off her spacecraft, the Earthlings became afraid that the higher beings of the universe had discovered their plan to rocket to other planets. Seizing Miss

Mongolia, they would make sure she would not tell the other aliens of their plan.

Miss Mongolia was sitting on the side of her bed when a woman unlocked the door and entered the room. The woman, who wore a small white triangular-shaped hat on her head, looked at Miss Mongolia, and then looked down. Even though very thin, Miss Mongolia was beautiful. The woman appeared to be very nervous as she left a tray of food on a table. She then turned to leave.

Miss Mongolia, surprised that the woman had not said anything to her, said, "Where am I?" The woman stopped at the door with her hand on the knob. It seemed that she would leave without answering, but she turned slightly and said, "You are in a hospital." Then she turned and quickly left the room, locking the door behind her.

Miss Mongolia was Vraman. Even though she was thirty-four years old, on Vrama, where the inhabitants live a life of thousands of years, Miss Mongolia would only be considered a child. Indeed, her body had not yet developed adult senses. And since her reasoning was still child-like, Miss Mongolia could not understand why anyone would want to hold her against her will.

Miss Mongolia walked past the food to the second door in the room. She found that the door was not locked, and behind it lay a bathroom, complete with toilet and shower.

After showering and redressing, Miss Mongolia investigated the food. There was a huge bowl of rice, several pieces of cheese, and two rolls of bread. There was a plastic spoon on the side of the bowl, but no knife or fork.

Miss Mongolia seated herself in the chair, picked up the spoon, and started on the rice. Where was her ship? After finishing her first mouthful of rice, Miss Mongolia lifted her head and said a mantra. With her eyes closed and deeply concentrating, Miss Mongolia moved her head to the right and then to the left. It wasn't anywhere. Her spaceship wasn't anywhere. And she was no longer on an island. She was now on a large continent.

Miss Mongolia opened her eyes. She picked up a roll and nibbled on it with intensity. She must recover her ship. But the barrier . . . How would she get through the barrier? Any Vraman would know, but the trick was to find one here on Earth.

Howee _____

Coalition Ingenu

Introduction by Robert Bullock

Coalition Ingenu was founded in 1995 to present an alternative to the art of formally trained artists who *depend upon* finding a market for their work. Coalition Ingenu artists are generally people who have little interest in fame or fortune, but who create art for the pure and simple experience of exploring their imaginations and realizing their personal visions. They do it for themselves. Many of them never cared about exhibit opportunities, possibly because they didn't think anyone would understand or appreciate their work. Coalition Ingenu believes the determination of these artists, in spite of their circumstances, lends power, honesty, and validity to their work.

Coalition Ingenu works with self-taught artists who are precluded from participation in the mainstream art community by circumstances of poverty or mental disability. Coalition Ingenu promotes their work by providing a variety of services, including: assembling portfolios; negotiating exhibit opportunities; framing (or otherwise preparing artwork for presentation); writing press releases; designing, printing and mailing announcements and other promotional materials; hanging the exhibits; planning receptions; advertising; and handling the proceeds from the sales of artwork.

Coalition Ingenu considers itself to be primarily an arts organization. Its artists are mostly recruited from art programs in mental health centers or homeless shelters, and most are considered legally disabled for one or more reasons. However, Coalition Ingenu does not focus on these issues, but on the abilities and unique expressive choices of the individuals it serves.

It is true that the process of creating artwork has inherent therapeutic benefits, and artmaking in a group environment promotes social interaction. Self-expression and creative activity may also help to facilitate the healing of emotional and psychic wounds. Following a project through to completion helps participants develop positive work habits and self-confidence. Inclusion in dignified art exhibits can improve self-esteem, and proceeds from sales provide artists with a little extra income. Coalition Ingenu facilitates open studio art classes at various locations to provide work spaces, supplies, and environments for these things to occur. But it has always been the assembling and arranging of exhibits, with the audience in mind, that has been the primary focus for the organization.

In short, Coalition Ingenu hopes to encourage its audience to appreciate rare and wonderful works of art that may have otherwise been discarded simply because the artists never had the opportunity to display them in a proper setting. The mission is simple: to give these works of art the presentation they deserve by virtue of the spirit in which they are created.

Over the course of their six-year history, Coalition Ingenu has built a following of art lovers and social service advocates alike. They have organized over 50 exhibits, worked with over 100 artists, displayed over 5,000 pieces of artwork, and collaborated with over 30 hospitals and nonprofits throughout the Delaware Valley. The exhibits range from all-inclusive group shows, to more selective and thematic exhibits of art by smaller groups.

Although the skills necessary to make art (as a commodity) can often be taught, learned, practiced, and developed, Coalition Ingenu has found that a unique style that comes directly from a complex, self-aware, and courageous personality cannot be contrived.

Our goal is to cultivate admiration for these qualities, and to celebrate the exclusive abilities and accomplishments of these artists, even if they do not fit squarely into the system of what is valued in our society.

The pictures on these pages represent a small sampling of the work of the most prolific, popular, and distinctive members of our group.

Vanise Clay

"Friends," Watercolors and ballpoint pen

"My Spot," Watercolors and ballpoint pen

Vanise Clay

"Frankie," Oil pastel crayons

George Johnson

"Song," Acrylics on canvas

George Johnson

"Monkey Man," Acrylics on canvas

John Author Goffigan

**Coalition
Ingenu**

100

"Holy Man," Tempera on paper

John Author Goffigan

"Goffigan Bird," Mixed media with clay

David Kime

"Pre-hysterics," Doll parts, wire, melted crayon

David Kime

"Pre-hysteric," Doll parts, wire, melted crayon

Ron Lellis

"Alexander Graham Bell," Pastels on black paper

Ron Lellis

"Self Portrait," Mixed media

And the Sun Still Shines

Tameka Blackwell

I love the sunlight that shines in on Thomas Jefferson Hospital's glass enclosed bridge.

The bridge has the appearance of hovering over Sansom Street. It was built as an extension for connecting the Chestnut Street side of Jefferson Hospital to the Walnut Street side. They once operated as two separate buildings. The Walnut Street side was built many years before the Chestnut Street side. Thomas Jefferson Hospital has become the premier hospital in the Northeast that handles spinal cord injuries. Anyhow, I'm glad it exists.

The elevators are full, as usual. Well, I'll have to wait for the next one, as usual. How dare these people delay my mission to the ninth floor, the purple floor, where my spot in the sun awaits me?

Purple is the color scheme of the floor — room numbers, nurses' stations, and the large number that greets you when the elevator doors open. The other floors have color schemes, too. The fifth floor is yellow, third floor is green, and the eighth floor is red.

Where are all these people coming from?

All right, I am forced to jock for position. 5. . . 4 . . . it's on its way down . . . 3 . . . 2 . . . you fools better move out my way . . . 1 . . . here I go — zoom. I love it.

Don't leave on my account.

Once I'm on the elevator people don't like to ride with me. They usually jump out to get in another elevator. Maybe I frighten them by moving so quickly? Well, if I didn't, people would never let me on. So fine, don't get on with me — fewer stops.

Mom pushes the number nine and away we go. Man, she looks so tired.

"Mom, I got a plan."
"Yeah. What?"
"I'm a start my story for Eli's class when I get on the bridge."
"Yeah. You said that for the past two weeks."
"I know. But today is the day."
"Uh huh."
"Listen. My appointment is not until . . . what, another hour or so? I can start writing now. Right?"
"Right . . . turn around straight. So you can get off without hitting the arm of that chair."
"I got it."
"Yeah."
 Man, she sounds tired. Bing!

The Ninth floor, sunshine here I come. Great, no one else is on the bridge. My three favorite elements for writing — and sleeping — sunshine and peace and quiet. Just as I like it.
"You need all three of your pillows?"
"Yes' um."
"Yes' um?"
"Thanks mom."
"Yes' um. I am going to sit in the lounge and it's about 11:00 o'clock. So come around about quarter of . . . 12."
 "How am I supposed to know that?"
It's funny, after so many years she still forgets about my inabilities.

"Oh, that's right. I'll come back at twenty of."

"OK."

"Don't fall asleep or daydream with all this sun."

"You know me too well."

She even walks tired.

All right, Let the Story Writing Begin. Or, Let My Story Begin. Yeah, that sounds better as a title. This sun feels so good. I like to just turn my face up to it.

The flashing red lights on that ambulance are so red. It's pulling into the Emergency and Trauma Unit on Tenth Street. That wasn't here, at Jefferson, when I was brought to this hospital. I wonder if the person inside's body is packed in ice for stabilization? As mine was. I wonder if they even do that anymore, after a person's been pronounced DOA? As I was. I wonder if they need a tube inserted in their tracheae so they can breathe? As I needed. I wonder if the person is being transferred here from another hospital because of the severity of their illness? As I was transferred here from another hospital that wasn't capable of handling a person with my level of spinal injury. Whew! What a ride, from then to now. Thank you, Jesus, for my Life.

"Hey, Tameka. Right?"

"Hi, Dr. Dittuno." A Spinal Cord Specialist and my doctor during my seven-month stay here.

I cannot believe this man is still here. Still wearing his glasses on the tip of his nose. Let me peek at the feet. Yup, the brown Stacey Adams turned up at the toes.

"How are you, sweetie? You look wonderful. Here for a tune up?"

I frown at the word "sweetie." I know I was young when I came here, but I am well past the sweetie stage. And I'm still processing the "tune up" remark. I left my house this morning promising myself not to become "Super Woman: The Crusader for all Causes." But, I can't help it.

"Sweetie, doc?"
"Oh yeah, how old are you now?"
"Too old for sweetie."

An awkward silence falls between us while he rocks back and forth on the worn heels of his shoes. Should I release him now, or let him squirm a little more? Oh, I'll dismiss him, only because he looks so uncomfortable and I have work to do. Besides, I can't hold in my laughter any longer and he's blocking my sun.

"Yup, here for a routine check up."
"OK then, see you later. Keep up the good work."
Laughter.

It amazes me how little common sense some of these doctors have. (Smile.)

I guess many people don't expect the things that come out of my face. Man, this sun feels nice. I'm glad that cloud is gone. I don't want any clouds on this beautiful sunny day. All right, back to my story.

Why is Mom coming now? It can't be 11:45 already. I only have drawings of sunny smiley faces on my page. I wanted to have at least three or four pages written before she came for me or I get back home. Watch she asks me how much I've written.

"How much did you write?"

"Aren't you early?"

"No, it's quarter of. That's all you did was draw pictures of smiley faces?"

"I'm still thinking."

"Yeah, OK. Do you want all this stuff put away?"

"No. But, listen. My brain juices are just getting started."

She smiles. "Yeah, all right. Get started around to the doctor's office."

Laughter.

I love her one-liners, and her smile. She doesn't look as worn out when she got a smile on her face.

I hate this office. I always have to skillfully maneuver my way around the Ikea-looking doctor's office furniture in order to find a corner to squeeze into while I wait my turn. There is a spot, between two cheaply framed chairs. It's about twenty-two inches wide. Thank goodness I'm twenty-one inches wide.

Then I only have to go through the same ritual to get out of the spot where I wedged myself in.

Not bad. I whipped myself right in here. You go BIG GIRL.

"The lady said Dr. Chinkins is running around thirty minutes late."

"OK. That'll give me time to write at least a page or two."

"Yeah, alright. Put everything back on you?"

"Mm, hm. Thanks."

"Mm hm."

Back to my empty page with the sunshine faces on it. Better yet, I'll start on a clean slate or clean page.

"You have an audience." Despite my mother leaning over to tell me this — she cannot whisper. I'm sure everyone in this matchbox of an office heard her.

I nod in agreement, before she loudly whispers something else.

Yes mommy, I'm aware of the woman across from me whose skin and attire look as if she just flew in from Florida. I know it's nice today, but sandals and puddle-pushers? Oh, excuse me, capris. Aren't you aware it's still March? I saw her when she came in. Try to ignore her and write. I have two pages of thoughts down. Don't stop the flow and do not look up again to meet her eyes – too late. No. Please don't stare. I do not feel like playing the staring game with you. I have work to do. And trust me, I am much better at it than you are. Just smile then.

Smile.

All right, the soft smile I gave you was a hint that you're being rude. It must've not worked because your eyes are still on me. I'm forced to give you the eye treatment. OK. What shall I focus on? Maybe your black roots that need a blonde touch up. Or maybe your thin red painted lips. No, not the lips. I'll wind up laughing before I'm finished treating you with my eyes. Found it. That blotchy sunburned forehead with its four deep creases has my full attention.

She looks and I look. She looks and I look. She looks and I look. She looks and I look. Has anyone ever told this intelligent woman how rude it is to stare?

The woman with the gold hoop earrings and the blue raincoat, a London Fog like my grandmother used to wear, sitting next to my sunburned friend, appears to understand the purpose of my eye treatment. She shakes her head in disgust. Raincoat lady got the message. She probably was taught the same lesson I was privileged to learn. "DO NOT STARE, it's rude and impolite."

She looks and I look. She looks and I look. She looks and I look. She looks and I look. Oh, great. You call my name now. I am just getting relaxed. Do I turn away now? NEVER!

"Come on Mekey." This is my affectionate family name given to me by my niece when she was two. She couldn't pronounce my name Tameka properly.

She looks and I look. She looks and I look. She looks and I look. I don't feel like being Super Woman and teaching this woman some manners.

"Come on, your chair is on." My mom's voice tells me she's fed up with this lady's rudeness and my response to it.

I rest my head on my headrest, with my eyes locked on her forehead. My chair lunges forward. I take my head off the headrest, stopping the chair right in front of the rude woman's feet. She jumps, lifting her feet off the floor.

"I don't know if anyone has ever told you, but staring at people is very rude."

The woman blinks her eyes rapidly and looks at me as if she is amazed that I can speak.

All right, lady, I heard you call me the first time. Getting out this tight spot was a lot easier than I thought it would be. Maybe I feel as if I got some-thing to prove. Or, I don't care whether I take a few of these cheap chairs with me, including the one Mrs. Florida is sitting in. Anyway, I got skills. "Hi, Tameka?"

"No, she's Tameka?"

"I'm Tameka Blackwell."

Where is Erica, who sat at this desk for the past five years? She knows who is who. I hate breaking in new people.

"Yes, Ms. Blackwell. Dr. Chinkins will not be able to see you today and apologizes for any inconvenience."

Silence.

Where is Erica? This woman sounds like a recording. BEEP, please hold. BEEP, press one.

"Are you having any problems with your toes? Are you diabetic?"

"No, no problems. Nor am I diabetic."

"Because you could see Dr. Freed."

Dr. Freed? Not hardly. He's the same quack that don't believe it's essential for a person with a spinal cord injury to have their nails cut regularly and properly.

"No, that's quite all right."

"Would you like to make an appointment for next week?"

"No, I'll just call. Thanks."

"Let's go Bo." This is the affectionate name I gave my mom after I turned twenty-five, in order to keep from calling her "Mommy" in public.

It is warm enough to sit outside. I'll start to write when I get back home. Well, I get to enjoy the sun a little more. Finally, I don't have to fight to get on the elevator. Man, everyone is out today. You can always tell when it's lunchtime and when it is getting warm. The sun feels so warm.

"I am going to sit over here."

"OK. I'm going to sit over there, where the sun is."

"Keep watch for your ride."

"All right."

Well, if I'm not going to write, I still can think, while I'm sitting here. I'm still not sure about how to put my story on paper and make it interesting. I am not a very exciting person. I don't do much of anything.

No, please don't sit over here. I am in a corner minding my business. Besides, my eyeballs are tired of staring. Also, this wooden and stone bench next to me doesn't look very comfortable. Great, just what I don't want.

"Hi, honey." At least this little osteoporosistic white haired lady has the decency to speak. But that usually means there will be a slew of questions that will usually follow the gesture of politeness.

"Hi."

"Sun feels good, huh."

"Yup."

"I bet it feels really good to *your* body?"

You bet right, lady.

"Yup."

No, don't move any closer. Can't you tell by my short answers that I don't want to talk? Please, lady, that's close enough. If I move back I won't be in the sun.

"Where do you live, honey?"

I knew you had questions. It didn't take you long, sister. I know you didn't come sit over here for the sake of sitting.

"North Philly."

"Oh, yeah, I heard about that place. A lot of dangerous things happening out there."

Now, before I come to the rescue of North Philly and scare the living daylights out this lady, let me process her idea of North Philly being somewhere afar or "out there."

"Were you born like that? Did something happen to you out there?"

Slow down, granny. I knew you were full of questions, but dag.

"I was shot."

I love to see people's facial response when I say that.

"Oh, my word."

Whew, I didn't know she had such beady little blue eyes behind all that hanging skin.

Silence.

I feel my mom's eyes on me. I'm not going to look in her direction.

I feel her eyes on me, just like those days when I was in church and talking with friends when I shouldn't have been. I would turn around to see her eyes chastising me.

Oh, I can't help it. Yup, she's looking at me.
Smile.

"Was it gang related?"

Oh, God, this woman watches too much TV. Her favorite is probably detective shows because she is one hell of an interrogator. But let me give her a dose of reality.

Super Woman to the rescue!

"No, my injury wasn't gang related. Actually, it didn't happen 'out there' in North Philly."

"Oh! Where did it occur?"

How did I know you were going to ask that?

"I was on the Boardwalk with some friends."

"The boardwalk? The Atlantic City Boardwalk?"

Look, lady, will you let me tell this story?

"No. It was the Ocean City Boardwalk . . . "
"Were you vacationing, school trip, just visiting? What?"
Man, Agatha Christie. Sit back on the edge of the bench and let me finish.
"Just visiting. And I was on the boardwalk and this man came over to me when I was laughing — I forget about what. Anyhow, he said, 'You know, you remind me of my wife.' Then as I began to leave or walk away, he shot me."
"My heavens! You poor dear. Well, did you look like his wife?"
Here comes the kicker.
"No, not at all. His wife was a thin woman with honey-blonde hair."
"What? What do you mean honey-blonde hair? You mean his wife was white?"
"Yup."
"Was he white too?"
"Uh, huh."
"Well, how did he think . . . "

"I don't know. I doubt if there were any similarities. Maybe it was my laugh. My mother used to tell me my laugh was going to get me in trouble."
Especially when I was in Catholic School.
"What happened to him?"
"It is said that he went three blocks and blew his brains out."
"Oh, no."
"Yup. No trial, no sentencing and no punishment."
"Where did he get the gun?"
"Oh, a small arsenal was later found in his home."

Silence.

Thank goodness someone is calling. This lady is full of questions.

She shakes her head and pats my arm. Then she

stands, while still shaking her head. She walks slowly toward a woman holding open a car door. The woman at the car has hair as gray as the inquisitive old lady, but her skin is considerably younger.

"Hey, Bo."
"What are you doing?"
"Why is it that you think I'm doing something?"
"Don't answer a question with a question. Besides, I know you."
"I wasn't doing anything but chit chatting."
"What did you say to that woman for her to go away shaking her head like that?"
"I told her what she wanted to know."
"What was that? What happened to you?"
"Yup, what else?"
"What did you say?"
"I told her all about my trip to Ocean City."
"Why you tell her that? You know that is not how you got injured."
"Because if I had told her that I was actually injured by a stray bullet from a police officer's gun who was running down my block and shooting at the back of a purse-snatching thief, she would not have felt the same despair about gun violence as she did hearing about my friend Eileen's shooting on the boardwalk.Or the story of Sharon's father shooting her because he thought she was a burglar. All my story does is confirm every stereotype about violence in North Philadelphia. And I'm sure my friends don't mind me sharing or borrowing their stories to make a point about the unexpectedness of gun violence."
"Maybe. But let people think what they want. What happened to you was no fault of yours. So who cares what they think? You are not the saving grace of North Philly."
"I know, but I can't help it sometimes."
"Well, when someone asks you what happened to

you, just say . . ."
"Ask me no questions and I'll tell you no lies."
"Yeah, that's good. Or tell them you'd rather not discuss it."
"I like mine better."
"Somehow I knew you would. I'm going inside to call and see why paratransit is late."
"All right."

When I get home on my porch I'll start my paper, for sure. Right after the double episode of *This Old House* goes off. I missed it last week when I was sitting in the sun and beginning my paper. Man, this sun is awesome.

"Hi."
"Hi. What is your name?"
"Thomas."
"My name is Tameka. How old are you?"
"6." He holds up six fingers. "Why are you sitting there?"

Super Woman to the rescue! I can't pass up an opportunity to teach little Thomas here about the dangers of guns. I better hurry up before my mother gets back.

"Well, my cousin was playing with a . . . ."

Deaf Culture
and the Birth of Creative Access

Text by Carol Finkle
Photos by Harvey Finkle

For as long as people have been Deaf and have communicated through the language of sign, there has been a Deaf culture. The depth and endurance of Deaf culture came to my husband and I when we had two Deaf children. What began with the limited perspective of deafness-as-hearing-loss, which viewed deafness solely as a medical condition, has evolved over the intervening twenty years to embrace the creative, the political, and the personal. Our evolved view holds that the medical fact of deafness is merely the foundation of a bona fide cultural identity, which our children and we have come to embrace and to celebrate. This is the story of that evolution.

The Deaf are the last oppressed minority because they have suffered the same indignities and oppression as numerous minorities throughout American history, and because of their invisibility.

Deaf people have historically been dominated by hearing individuals, the most notorious being Alexander Graham Bell, who sought to destroy Deaf culture and eradicate what the cultural anthropologists define as a mirror of any culture, its language. Bell was an oralist, who felt that Deaf people should learn to approximate speech to the exclusion of hand signing. This effort paralleled a similar eradication program of the late 19th Century — to purge the country of all that was Native American. These campaigns were spurred by superficial interpretations of the new Darwinian theories regarding the "purity of the gene pool," or eugenics. Bell himself sought legislation to deny marital rights to deaf people, foolishly believing that this would wipe out deafness once and for all. Deaf schools, the bastions of the culture, were closed, Deaf teachers fired, and American Sign Language forbidden, with severe punishments for any child caught using it. Some say this long, dark period (1880-1960), dominated by misguided, but well-intentioned hearing professionals, ended only when Deaf people took charge of their lives, driving out the colonialists, and establishing hegemony in their own right.

By the 1960's, the literacy rate for Deaf Americans, among the most literate groups in the country prior to the Bell initiatives, had plummeted. The overwhelming majority were reading at a third grade level. At this time, the first treatise establishing American Sign Language as a true language was published. William Stokoe's landmark work gave credence to what Deaf people have always known, and chipped away at the self-serving espousals of the Bell oralists. A new breed of educators began referring to Total Communication, a system which again recognized that normal first-language acquisition for most deaf children is visual.

With the arrival of American Sign Language in most schools for the Deaf across the country, Deaf culture itself became acknowledged, and celebrated, and its history part of any curriculum. Creation of the National Association of the Deaf and initiation of events like the Miss Deaf America pageant and the Deaf Olympics slowly but steadily led to a renewed sense of empowerment of Deaf people. Eventually, a popular revolt ended the long reign of hearing domination.

The most visible moment in this revolution came in the form of the Deaf President Now movement at Gallaudet University in 1988. Students (including our own) shut down the nation's only liberal arts university for the Deaf, the "Mecca" of Deaf education in the world. Students and alumni challenged the appointment by a patronizing board of directors of yet another hearing president of the school, by seizing physical control of the University. Gallaudet remained in a state of siege until the hearing appointee withdrew, and the first Deaf President in the hundred year history of the school took his place.

In the same time that it is said to have taken God to create the universe and all within, this uprising managed to dismantle the holy trinity of forces which dominated the lives of Gallaudet students for at least a century: Gone were the hearing chair, board, and president. On the heels of this upswing in pride I witnessed over the intervening years, my determination to enlighten my own City to wake up and take notice began to germinate.

CALL TO ACTION

In the spring of 1991 Creative Access was born. The Americans with Disabilities Act had been enacted one year prior, yet, for the most part,

Deaf people were still invisible and excluded from the general social and cultural life around me. Ramps and restrooms for the physically disabled seemed to be everywhere, but nary a sign language interpreter in sight. My battle cry today is "Interpreters equal ramps." "Captioning equals ramps!" "Communication is a basic human right!" But in 1991 we still couldn't go to the movies as a family (no captions), still couldn't take in a Broadway show (no interpreters), and most well endowed arts education programs were still marketed to hearing children only. The hearing world can't imagine life without art, yet our arts-starved Deaf children and families were barely noticed.

I saw that the reason there was an entire mental health industry devoted solely to people with hearing loss was directly related to this fact — i.e., that the concomitant social isolation, resulting from near-total exclusion from the social and cultural life of the dominant society, was at the root of a pervasive depression which I observed across the Deaf world like a sad, intangible veil. In a phrase, life was no fun, something I could identify with completely after twenty-some years of opening the Weekend section of the Philadelphia *Inquirer* and finding not a single thing for our family to participate in, look forward to, or enjoy.

Creative Access's mission is to change Philadelphia from a City whose arts life has for so long been closed off to the Deaf and their hearing families, into a model of what I refer to as "accessibility beyond the ramp." If invisibility was at the root of the marginalization and isolation that Deaf people experienced, then visibility was key to eroding stereotypes and reversing that picture. "What's the best way to do this?" There are two goals: access to and inclusion in the arts, and creation of a Deaf Committee on Human Rights!

The things that hurt most during all of my children's growing up years were that they couldn't go to movies or to the theater. As they grew, we approached the time when they, instead of being Deaf children, denied of the instructive, inspirational and curative benefits of the arts, would become the Deaf moms and dads, whose families would still be left out! So I took on Hollywood, went straight to presenters of great Broadway shows and cutting edge plays, and linked arms with myriad other disenfranchised groups that had similar, more overtly political agendas.

Creative Access, with a majority Deaf board, knocked on every door in the arts community (theaters, presenters, museums, the ballet), showing them the need. Then we built coalitions to tap into the "strength in numbers" factor. Lastly, we partnered with all who were agreeable, struggling with those who were not, when necessary. Sometimes we organized old-fashioned, in-your-face public demonstrations, like those in front of major movie theaters, to bring home the exclusion of Deaf and hard of hearing Americans from the single most popular choice of entertainment in the world.

And the struggle continues on all fronts. Hollywood, for example, in a mean-spirited maneuver, got itself exempted from the very mandate of the Americans with Disabilities Act that ensured people with disabilities were treated as full citizens, and that access to and inclusion in every part of American life was their right (not a privilege). The theater community has been a bit more accommodating, often open to the notion of inviting a new audience to the theater.

Beyond access to the world of hearing arts, there is another essential aspect to Creative Access's vision. As often is the case, the one is necessary but not sufficient. We want not only to ensure that the world of hearing arts is made accessible to my children and their peers, but also to create opportunities which showcase the talent of Deaf performing artists, who present their art form through the magic of American Sign Language for all audiences. Of all Creative Access programs, it is this, the Deaf Performing Artists Initiative, of which I am most proud, and which is the most beloved across the communities Creative Access serves. The reason is obvious: the pride inherent in seeing "your own kind" on stage, in a performance celebrating your culture. These artists are role models for generations of Deaf children, who see Deaf artists perform, achieve and excel. The message is clear. The world of theatre arts is for ALL people. It is interesting to note that American Sign Language, once seen as a symbol of shame and failure, forbidden, pushed underground and in danger of extinction, has become the single most valued display of pride, worn as a badge of honor, by Deaf people everywhere.

The battle for acknowledgement, access and inclusion continues to be an uphill one, with old, familiar forces waiting in the shadows to erode our progress as fast as we achieve it. Recently, several episodes shed light on the need for continued struggle by Deaf Americans.

First, there was the superintendent of a New Jersey school district who forbid a Deaf child to use sign language on her school bus, claiming that signing was disruptive. Next, a noted local art critic publicly condemned the provision of sign interpretation at a Broadway production of "Les Miserables," claiming it was a stupid and wasted effort since the Deaf can't hear music anyway. This was somewhat amusing in that his comments revealed his own ignorance and made it obvious that he had never seen Deaf children dance, or witnessed how much they love the lyrics, even when they can "read" them through sign or captions. Most recently, the respected Superintendent (Deaf) of the Riverside School for the Deaf was removed from her position because the hearing power structure disagreed with her policies regarding hiring and curriculum. In fact, the very survival of many Deaf schools across the country is now threatened. The most recent scenario was in North Carolina. As did many before them (and no doubt many will yet follow suit) North Carolina decided that one great way to deal with their state's budget crunch was to get rid of the Deaf school.

The arts have proven to be an effective vehicle for promoting social change and the rights of Deaf Americans. By bringing Deaf performers and audiences into the cultural mainstream, we can significantly enhance consciousness about their existence, their rights, their capabilities and potential contributions. Further, access to the arts adds yet another hue to the already rich and diverse face of our cities. In the first paragraph, I referred to things which have proven true throughout history. Another of those truths is that when groups who are different come out of the shadows and into the mainstream, everybody wins. If, in the end, what one recent Mayor of Philadelphia and the recent Governor of Pennsylvania claim is also true — i.e., "the arts are an essential ingredient for the quality of life of every citizen, and without it that quality of life is diminished" — then, I say — Hear, hear (sign, sign)! The arts have long proven to be the inspirational nutrition of the soul, the veritable antidote to oppression. So, let there be art, for all!

Photography by Harvey Finkle

Protesters from the Philadelphia and NW Ohio Deaf and Deaf Blind Committee on Human Rights join thousands for a march down Broad Street to the Republican National Convention. July, 2000.

Deaf bicyclist from US team. Deaf Olympics, Christchurch, New Zealand, 1989.

Deaf women from every state compete during Miss Deaf America pageant. Indianapolis, Indiana, July, 1990.

CJ (Charles) Jones, acclaimed Deaf actor/comedian, and a young fan sign "thank you" to each other after CJ's sold out performance before a mixed Deaf/hearing audience. American Sign Language and "Voice" at the Philadelphia ArtsBank, Winter, 1996. Part of Creative Access's Deaf Performing Artists Initiative.

Deaf wedding. Connecticut, 1994.

Deaf athletes at World Games for the Deaf (Deaf Olympics) during supper. Sign languages from around the world being shared. Christchurch, New Zealand, 1989.

Art and Visual Impairment

Artmaking complements sensory impairment, because it enhances the individual capacity for communication. As an essentially tactile form, sculpture readily lends itself to expression and appreciation for people who are Blind or have visual impairments.

The artists featured on the following pages have participated in two long-running art programs for the visually impaired. Since 1971, the Philadelphia Museum of Art has offered Form in Art, a weekly studio program for the Blind and visually impaired. Under the leadership of professional artists Eiko Fan and Vaughn Stubbs, participants in this program have produced thousands of works, which have been exhibited at the Museum, at Wills Eye Hospital, and in Tokyo and Kobe, Japan. Form in Art has received several awards, including the 2001 Louis Braille Award from the Associated Services for the Blind.

Vision thru Art is a sculpture class for legally Blind adults, coordinated by Robert Fluhr at the Allens Lane Art Center in Philadelphia's Mt Airy neighborhood. Fluhr emphasizes the community-building nature of artmaking, "We are a group of artists and volunteers that promotes tolerance, understanding, and respect for differences in an informal, creative, environment.

"Bear," Michael Geisher

Betsy Clayton

Andrea Mullock

"Family Outing," Romaine Samworth

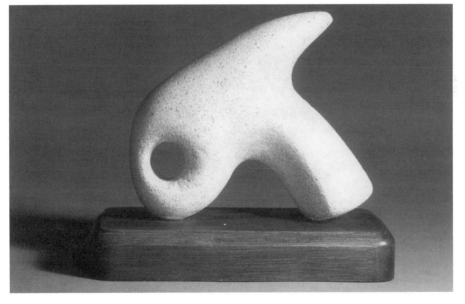

Tom Maddin

Martina Webb

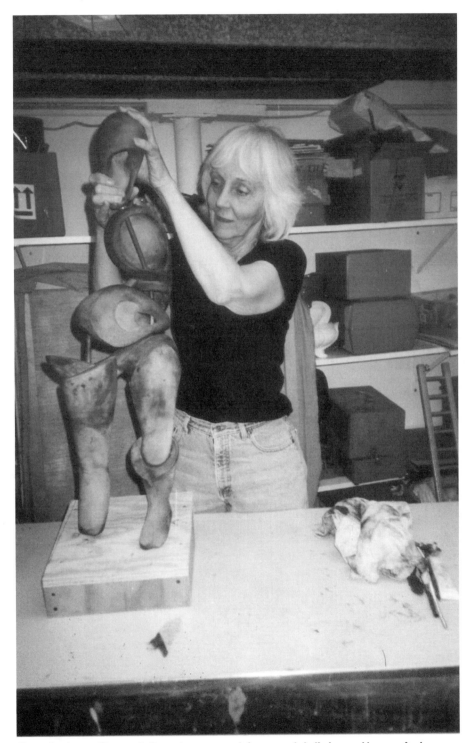

Sculptor Carol Saylor working at Vision thru Art

Alike Angels of Old

Michelle Suzette Patente

You lay in your bed
calling on death against your will
when a voice inside of you spoke
reminding you we are but visitors

Still, death did not want you
and you were glad

the golden birds came unto you
they carried you between their wings
alike angels of old
they soaked you in great cool waters
until you were well
then, they flew you back to your bed

The others did not believe your story
they never do

Thoughts on a Theater Class

Barbara Gregson

The two men dressed in black, Jerome and Richard, both in their 40's, both with beards, crouch down, bending over at the waists side by side, their faces looking downwards, their middle arms lifelessly resting next to each other, giving support to each other, their outside arms and bodies slowly rising up from that crouched position, growing, to form branches of a tree. Their torsos, legs and inside arms the trunk of the tree, their outside arms and fingers gracefully moving above their heads, standing together now, side by side. They breathe together, swaying along the with the music, (bells, chimes and cricket sounds played by musicians) their branches being blown by a soft summer breeze . . . .

Alice, 60, enters a toy store, observes the stuffed animals, but passes them by, to become enthralled by a large doll. Christina, 47, who is wearing a floppy hat and a ruffled dress, is sitting in a chair, sort of propped up, and frozen like a large doll. The woman caresses her and moves her stiff limbs for her. The doll starts to move and comes alive, to the woman's joy and surprise. The woman buys her, the doll stands and does a little doll dance, and the woman walks off with her as the doll dances off. Alice recites the Japanese haiku: "A childless housewife tenderly caresses the new dolls for sale . . . ."

Jacquie, 60, drives. She sits in a wheelchair, moving only one arm as she drives. Her grown son, Jerome, is in the back seat as the car starts. He tells her, "Ma, I don't want you picking up any hitchhikers today. Remember what Dad said." She answers him with a smile and happily hums to herself as she drives. (Jaquie cannot use words but communicates brilliantly by using gestures, sounds and facial expressions.) She sees a man by the side of the road, and stops and beckons for him to come in. Jerome yells, "Ma, what are you doing! I told you no more hitchhikers, Ma!" She just smiles, hums and happily drives. The hitchhiker sits in the front seat and begins to give orders, like, "Take me down the road 50 miles, turn up the radio, etc." He becomes increasingly bossy and rude. The more the son protests, the more the mother keeps driving along smiling and singing and gesturing to the son to be quiet, ignoring him, and getting along better and better with the hitchhiker. The action builds to the point where Jacquie stops the car, and the hitchhiker and Mother kick the son out of the car and go on their merry way, humming along. The audience roars with laughter and applause . . . . And the show ends.

These are descriptions of a few of the theater pieces and improvisations that were performed by 12 actors for live audiences at Magee Rehabilitation, in Philadelphia, after participating in a series of theater classes during September, 2000 to June, 2001. The actors studied mime, acting, improvisation, playwriting, mask making, and set design, then created three original shows for performance. They were accompanied by a professional musician. The actors weren't any different from other beginning adult theater students that I have taught except for the fact that they were physically disabled. Several of the students had suffered violent injuries, such as car accidents or gunshot wounds, and others had had strokes or brain injuries that left them with some form of paralysis. A few students had had cerebral palsy since childhood. Many of the students had some type of difficulty speaking, writing or remembering words, and many used a wheelchair, cane or walker to get around. What I loved about the class was the tremendous diversity of ages – eighteen to sixty-five — and backgrounds. They came from all over Philadelphia and the surrounding area.

Once, as an outsider, in a country in which I didn't speak the language — German — I joined an avant-garde theater company called "Rost" (Rust). The actors gave me all of the non-verbal movement parts, which was actually a relief and enabled me to focus on just the movement, rather than worry about my German pronunciation. While working with this company, I tried very hard to decipher the language. I would concentrate intensely, and imagine what they were saying, by looking at the facial expressions and body language, tone of voice, or any other clues. I used parts of my brain that I never had used before. Then of course when I tried to speak, I would use gestures, bad sign language, mime, and whatever I could think of to get my point across. I eventually ended up in Paris, in another country where I didn't speak the language, which led me to study mime.

Teaching a theater class with people with disabilities reminds me of those years living in those foreign countries. All of us in the class are foreigners trying to understand each other's words or gestures. In the beginning, there is no common language. We will find it, but first we must learn to communicate with one another, and to find out how each one expresses himself or herself. We begin by thinking like artists. As Robert Alexander, Director of the Living Stage Theatre Company, said, "An artist is someone who cares passionately about communicating."

It is our goal to think like artists and to bring our ideas and individual artistry across to a live audience. Like everyone, the students in the class have physical limitations. Particular theater techniques and arts practices highlight their strengths, and at the same time push the actors to use parts of their bodies they aren't accustomed to using. How can we show a feeling, character, or dramatic expression, how tell a story and its essence with a hand gesture, a facial expression, eyes, one arm? By learning mime. Not the clichéd whiteface, white glove mime that is shallow and predictable, but by studying what mime really means: mime is maximum idea with minimum movement.

After exploring mime techniques, which they can use to tell their stories, participants collaborate with each other and create original dramatic/mime pieces, from improvisations, Japanese haiku or adapted pieces from folktales. They express meaningful ideas with the simplest and yet most dramatic movement, sometimes adding voice, live music and masks.

While cutting our foam core set and painting it during several rehearsals, I asked the actors about their feelings during theater class. Richard said, "Taking the theater class makes me feel a lot less afraid. When I first had a stroke I was afraid to go out and walk down the street. People treated me like a baby. But now I feel a lot more confident, and I like being able to express myself in this way." Alice said, "It helps me to stand up in front of people and speak. I also love the interactions with the other people." Using his assistive speech device, Robbie said, "I love it! I'll be back next September." Brenda said the classes helped to give her more self-confidence. We actually called her "the director" by the end of the classes, as she came right out and said what the actors should do over or what wasn't clear. With a beautiful hand gesture, the sound of her voice, and her facial expression, Jacqui showed us that she was sad and frustrated at times that she couldn't speak words, yet at least the classes gave her an outlet to express herself.

"Silence: The butterfly sleeps on the chapel bell." Center stage, Darlene spoke this haiku clearly, slowly and with great diction. Though she had originally had trouble remembering words and how to say them, she could finally articulate them very well. Renette came on stage, and Darlene moved to stage right. Renette moved with large steps, swaying slightly. She looked around as she entered, as though in a forest. The music began with sounds of wind chimes, flute, and the wind. Darlene said, "Renette was walking in the forest one day and she found a butterfly." Renette's discovery of an imaginary butterfly conveyed such awe and concentration that we too saw it. She made short, staccato movements, interspersed with larger swoops of her head. Then Richard came, and also saw the butterfly. Richard slowly joined Renette. They both watched the butterfly with intensity. Their movements were exactly the same, though they could not see each other as they were standing side by side. The butterfly was red and blue. It was the most beautiful butterfly they ever saw. They watched it with total synchronization. The other actors started to come on stage individually and in pairs. All twelve were on stage, watching the butterfly. Renette tried to catch it and it flew off lazily. Everyone continued watching it as it went off stage right. Darlene said, "It's gone." Everyone watched it leave, then paused, and turned back to face the audience with a collective sigh. The End.

Barbara Gregson (left, front) with the cast and crew of the Magee Players. Photo by Josh Robinson.

Soundtrack

Suzanne Bacal

My eyes snap awake.
What time is it?
(Don't look or you'll know how few hours are left
        to sleep.)
Light parallelograms dance on my dark ceiling.
No, the sun has not yet begun to rise.

> The heee-whoosh, heee-whoosh of my
>   Magic Machine
> beats an easy rhythm in the dark silent
>   night.

Snatches of my life run through my mind like
closed-captioning: Will my personal assistance
arrive on time? Will my transportation be there at
8:00? Did I settle that problem at the office or will
I have to revisit it today?

> The heee-whoosh, heee-whoosh of my Magic
>   Machine
> repeats its nightly rhumba.

My position is fine.
My breathing is fine.
No inner-city sounds tonight.

All is well.

> The heee-whoosh, heee-whoosh, heee-
>   whoosh of my Magic Machine
> soothes me with its steady cadence.

Oh bother.
The morning will come without the necessity of
my taking control.

> Heee-whoosh, heee-whoosh, heee-whoosh.

Contributors Notes

Rodney Atienza is a documentary photographer who focuses on issues of social concern. His work has included documentation of homelessness, disability issues, and struggles for justice within various Philadelphia communities. For information about his work, visit www.RJAPhoto.com or call 215.509.6785

Suzanne Bacal was the Chair of the Mayor's Commission on People with Disabilities, and Director of Educational Programs at Liberty Resources. At the time of her death in early 2001, she was the longest-tenured employee at Liberty. Perhaps her most significant memorial was the August 30, 2000, victory in U.S. District Court forcing SEPTA ParaTransit to comply with the ADA, a suit which Suzanne initiated.

Tameka Blackwell is a C-4 quadriplegic born and raised, and living in Strawberry Mansion, North Philadelphia. Since the age of 12 she has had a passion for telling stories, both fiction and non-fiction (often mixing the two), to express the often-misunderstood worlds of: Black, Female, North Philadelphia, and Disability.

Victoria A. Brownworth is an award-winning journalist, author of seven books and editor of ten. A former columnist for the Philadelphia *Daily News*, her writing appears in many national publications in both the queer and mainstream press, including *Ms.*, the *Village Voice*, the *Baltimore Sun*, the *Bay Area Reporter*, and the Philadelphia *Inquirer*. Her writing on disability has appeared in many publications, including *Disability Studies*

Quarterly. She teaches writing and film at the University of the Arts.

Founded in 1995 by self-taught artist **Robert Bullock**, **Coalition Ingenu** works to promote and encourage creativity as a means to psychological and emotional well-being; and to create a complete system for the recognition of outstanding creative expressions by self-taught artists with histories of homelessness, mental disability, or physical limitations.

Alan Catlin has been publishing in small press and university literary magazines for over twenty-five years. His work has been nominated thirteen times for Pushcart prizes, he has won several chapbook contests and is awaiting the publication of his selected poems from Pavement Saw Press.

Maria Dewan is a graduate of Temple University with a B.A. in Psychology. She lives in a Center City apartment where she reads, writes and enjoys living life on her own terms.

Jim DeWitt is the author of 34 published books. He is a language researcher that served as president of the Michigan Council of Teachers of English, directed six annual youth writing competitions, and participated in the Creative Writers in the Schools Program of the Michigan Council for the Arts.

Carol Finkle is a hearing parent of two Deaf children, has two M.A. degrees in the field of Deafness and is the Founder and Executive Director of Creative Access, a Philadelphia based non-profit organization using the realm of the arts for social change since 1992.

Harvey Finkle is a documentary still photographer whose interests are social, political and cultural. His work includes documenting Deaf culture, refugees and immigrants, poor peoples movements, and other activities related to social movements.

Nellie Greene is a graduate of Hampshire College and Yale Divinity School. A Deacon in the Episcopal Church, she currently serves at the Methodist Church, in Chestnut Hill, Philadelphia.

Beth Greenspan is a published poet and photographer living in a supported apartment program in Ardmore, PA. She is thirty-eight years old and has been struggling with brain disabilities all of her life. With a lot of assistance and medications, she leads an unconventional life selling cards of her flower photography and keeping active with her many interests and collections.

Barbara Gregson studied Theatre in London, England and mime in Paris, France in the 70's and mask making in Italy in the 90's. She has lived in Philadelphia, PA since 1980, performing, teaching and creating original productions with people of all ages and abilities in diverse cultural settings. Barbara has been an artist in education with Pennsylvania Council on the Arts since 1984.

Gabrielle Howee was born in 1967. She has lived in Philadelphia all of her life. Her interests are writing and painting in watercolor.

David Kime is a 35 year old writer, sculptor and

human rights activist. He loves listening to music and relaxing in his Levittown apartment.

Jessie Jane Lewis' work is represented in important art collections both here and abroad. Her videos and performances have been broadcast nationally on cable university channels as well as locally on Channel 12. Longtime member and past president of Nexus Foundation for Today's Art, Philadelphia, Lewis directed the citywide Bodyworks project (1994) and now works for EQUAL ACCESS NOW, an advocacy effort focusing on voter rights. Ms. Lewis extends her thanks to **Janice Merendino** for layout design assistance with "Signs of Protest."

Donnie Means uses his words in poetry and prose to act as tentacles so that he can reach the human psyche of common bonds and grounds. He writes to remind others that having a disability doesn't mean that you are incapable of giving, sharing, learning and growing like everyone else.

B.Z. Niditch is the artistic director of The Original Theatre in Boston. His work appears in *Columbia: A Magazine of Poetry and Art*, *The Literary Review*, *Denver Quarterly* and *Hawaii Review*.

Scott Norman's interest in literary craft is a direct outgrowth of his disability. Survivor of the psychiatric system since age 14. Now studying alternative medicine. Never completed ninth grade. Studied poetry at college level with Stephen Dunn.

Gil Ott is the Editor and Publisher of Singing Horse Press, and is the author of twelve books of poetry and fiction. He is Director of Development for Liberty Resources.

Michelle Suzette Patente is a French-Ukranian American orphan-poet, street-writer and social reformer. She has been writing for twenty-seven years in the heart of downtown Philadelphia. The author's royalties from "The Flower Man" and her other works, "The Glass Pimper" and "My Father was a Frenchman," are dedicated to social reform.

chriss-spike quatrone has discarded all of the labels that others have imposed on her. She delights in her writing, her work, and walking in the woods.

Joe Randell flunked English in the 12th grade. His teacher wrote on Joe's report card that "He sits there with a 'to hell with it' look on his face." He graduated in 1977, and in 1979 had an acute schizophrenic episode. Since his hospitalization he has struggled to stay out of the hospital. Presently Joe is taking 7 different medications for his mind. His doctor and he have been experimenting with a drug called Seroquel. Joe isn't sure if he has an anxiety disorder or a schizophrenic thought disorder.

Bonnie Schell, MA, has managed a drop-in center with writing classes in Santa Cruz, CA since 1994. Bonnie edits the Poetic Justice column for *MindFreedom Journal*, was editor of the *Cal Net Gazette* for four years, and organizes readings by people who have had a madness experience. She was co-editor of *Reaching Across with the Arts*.

Sieglinde A. (Sigi) Shapiro consults on and teaches disability policy at Temple University. She has advocated for disability rights since 1973 and

Chairs the PA Advisory Committee to the U.S. Commission on Civil Rights. Her article is dedicated to the memory of Mimi Nelken who died in February, 2002.

Erik von Schmetterling is a 49 year old Gay Deaf man who has physical and mental disabilities, and who uses a motorized wheelchair. Before the start of his Disabilities, he was a physician, studying Cardiology and Emergency Room Medicine. In 1989, he became a member of ADAPT. Erik lives in Center City Philadelphia with his spouse of ten years, Jimmi Shrode.

Greg Wyatt has been an art teacher in St. Louis public schools for over a decade. His hobbies are cartooning and collecting Tiki mugs. Greg's favorite movie is "Santa Claus Conquers the Martians."

Thanks to the following individuals, who supported publication of *No Restraints*

Marjorie Backup
Iris Boshes
Lawrence Brick
Joyce Burd
Joan Carey
Mark A. Davis
Karin DiNardi
Thomas Earle, Esq.
Beverly Frantz
Fran Fulton
Lisa Gilden
Stephen Gold
Steven Green
James Hennessey
Charlene Hoffman
Marie Inyang
John Kane
Lawrence Kovnant
Larry Marr
Donald McCoy
Pam McGonigle & Katie Edgar
Patrick McGovern
Robert E. Michaels
Gil Ott
Ami Profeta
Deborah Russell
Spitfire Sabel
Jeffrey and Liz Thul
Jorja Urbansky
Vision for Equality
Maureen Wright

Steve Gold and Teresa Yates.
Photo by Harvey Finkle.

New City Press is committed to linking the personal stories and neighborhood histories of Philadelphia residents to meaningful movements for economic, educational, and social change. The Press has a special relationship with the neighborhoods around Temple University in North Philadelphia, but is also committed to empowering diverse voices in self-identified communities throughout the city. Our goal is to provide community writers with access to a larger audience, as well as to assist activists in bettering living conditions in urban neighborhoods. To that end, we work with established community and school projects which attempt to bear witness to and record neighborhood histories and support those who are collecting or developing narratives and stories of community members. We help to establish and shepherd writing groups in which such narratives can flourish, and work with teachers and community educators to discover ways in which writing can become a part of a public education movement.

Liberty Resources, Inc. is the Center for Independent Living for the Philadelphia area, which advocates for and works with Persons with Disabilities to ensure their civil rights and equal access to all aspects of life in our community.